COMMUNITY PRACTICE SKILLS WORKBOOK

Marie Weil, Dorothy N. Gamble,
and Emily R. MacGuire

COMMUNITY PRACTICE SKILLS WORKBOOK

LOCAL TO GLOBAL PERSPECTIVES

COLUMBIA UNIVERSITY PRESS ■ NEW YORK

COLUMBIA UNIVERSITY PRESS
Publishers Since 1893
New York   Chichester, West Sussex

Library of Congress Cataloging-in-Publication Data

Weil, Marie, 1941–
    Community practice skills workbook : local to global perspectives / Marie Weil,
Dorothy N. Gamble, and Emily R. MacGuire.
        p.   cm.
    ISBN 978-0-231-15133-7 (pbk. : alk. paper)
    1. Community-based social services.   2. Community organization.   3. Community
development.   I. Gamble, Dorothy N.   II. MacGuire, Emily.   III. Title.
    HV40.W388   2009
    361.8 — dc22   2009029618

We dedicate this book to the students who will use it, and to

Nathan Charles Weil
Andrew Winkelman
and
members of ACOSA who are committed to sharpening the skills of community practice workers the world over

CONTENTS

List of Illustrations   ix
Acknowledgments   xi
Introduction   xiii

PART I   **1**

1 Communities and Community Practice in Local to Global Contexts   7

2 Conceptual Frameworks and Models for Community Practice   10

3 Evolution of Values, Concepts, and Community Practice Approaches   16

4 Theories and Perspectives for Community Practice   23

PART II   **29**

5 Neighborhood and Community Organizing   31

6 Organizing Functional Communities   43

7 Social, Economic, and Sustainable Development   49

8 Inclusive Program Development   59

9 Communities and Social Planning   75

10 Building Effective Coalitions   88

11 Political and Social Action   96

12 Movements for Progressive Change   101

13 The Challenges for Community Practice Ahead   107

ILLUSTRATIONS

FIGURES

FIGURE W7.1. Hart's Community Capital Triangle — 57

FIGURE W7.2. Human Interaction toward Sustainability — 58

FIGURE W8.1. Community Practice Self-Assessment
Dimensions Reflection — 62

FIGURE W8.2. Logic Model for Promoting Maternal and Infant
Health in Rural Niger — 70

FIGURE W8.3. Proposed Program Budget: Promoting Maternal
and Infant Health in Rural Niger — 71

FIGURE W8.4. Program Timeline for Promoting Maternal and Infant
Health in Rural Niger — 72

FIGURE W10.1. Structure for a People's Hearing — 93

TABLE

TABLE W3.1. Ife's Categories of Human Rights — 21

ACKNOWLEDGMENTS

We acknowledge with grateful thanks the many students and colleagues who over the years have challenged our thinking, asked wonderful questions, and encouraged our work. We offer special appreciation to the following people:

To Paul Castelloe, Karen Smith Rotabi, Chin Jiagang, Kevin Branch, Evelyn Williams, Mat Despard, Thomas Watson, Dipanwitha Bhattacharyya, Ellen Netting, Mary Catherine O'Connor, David Fauri, Tesita Negussie, Anirudh Krishna, John Friedmann, Roland Bunch, Sarah Axelson, Nominise Gogo, Joan Pennell, Ivan Parra, Sara K. Price, Jim Ife, Beth Reed, Ben Warner, Janet Finn, Maxine Jacobson, Mac Legerton, Peter Medoff, Holly Sklar, Seth Maid, and Stephen Wiseman, who created case studies or materials that we have used in *Community Practice Skills: Local to Global Perspectives* and in *Community Practice Skills Workbook.*

To colleagues Claire Robbins, Nicole Keifer, Sarah Covington Kolb, Seema Varma, Evonne Lack Bradford, Emilie Brown, Mary Beth Cox Brown, Cherisa Frasier Hughes, Melissa Hafner Breaden, and Zach Rowles, who worked with us during their MSW careers, we offer particular thanks for their diligent research and support in helping us prepare for this book.

To Margaret Morse, Jennie Vaughn, Michelle Hughes, and Elizabeth Yerkes, whose fine editorial eyes and keen insights have strengthened our work over the years.

To former students, now colleagues, Wilburn Hayden, Robin Mauney, Jong-Gyu Paik, Chris Estes, Andrea Meier, Andrea Bazan Manson, Easter Maynard, Daniel Lebold, Ashley Montague, Jay Hemingway-Foday, Dana Courtney, Craig White, Sasha Vrtunski, Josh Prokopy, Melissa Johnson, Josh Hinson, Hope Morasco, Holly Yeager, Monica Haines, Melissa Sharer, Jim Lowder, Amily McCool, Mary Rider, Katie Rossini, Mary Beth Sullivan, Eric Simanis, Christina Wegs, and Anna Scheyett, whose encouragement has been invaluable and whose own work continues to inspire us.

INTRODUCTION

Welcome to *Community Practice Skills Workbook: Local to Global Perspectives* by Marie Weil, Dorothy N. Gamble, and Emily R. MacGuire. The textbook will broaden your knowledge about community practice by examining values, knowledge, theories, and eight current models that have diverse scope and related but distinctive goals for practice with communities. *Community Practice Skills (CPS)* highlights and explains skill areas necessary for effective work across a range of community practice modalities. The workbook builds on the textbook's discussion of skills and competencies for community practice and provides you with numerous direct exercises, role plays, discussion, and project ideas to deepen your skills and knowledge. These exercises allow you to practice ways to combine knowledge with action to effectively support and facilitate progressive community change through organizing, planning, and development work.

The goals for this workbook complement the *CPS* text and are designed to

- Increase and deepen your skills in community practice.
- Engage you with questions that relate practice with theory.
- Provide a range of active learning experiences that can be used with groups in class, in field settings, and in your practice career.
- Provide ways to analyze issues and synthesize new knowledge, interactive learning activities, and strategies to effectively incorporate new skills into your ongoing practice.

The interactive work recommended will include class discussions, exercises and activities, reflection papers, position taking on issues, and analysis of case studies. You will be asked to consider the actions of community practitioners and the groups they work with and to analyze strategy options you prefer to use.

A range of small-group and larger-group exercises are presented to take issues, ideas, and practice situations from the abstraction of text to the reality of practice. These practice simulations will focus on core skills related to empowerment strategies, group facilitation, developing and employing participatory planning, and using structured group decision-making processes. Strategies for group problem solving, and planning for and taking action to promote social justice and human rights are emphasized. You will also be asked to develop brief reflection papers on challenging issues as well as more complex individual and group activities, practice tools, and processes. You will be engaged in simulations of advocacy strategies, program and broader social planning, sustainable development, organizing, coalition development, and social action practice. We will provide you with links to related social and community issues and Web-based resources—all intended to strengthen skills you have already honed in your practice and to explore and test out skills in areas with which you are less familiar.

Many exercises were developed specifically for this workbook; others were selected from learning activities that we have used, tested, and adapted through our teaching/training experiences; still others were adapted from training manuals, and their sources are cited. We are particularly grateful that several case studies and exercises were developed by current and former students: Emily MacGuire, Seth Maid, Stephen Wiseman, Sarah Axelson, Karen Smith Rotabi, Tesita Negussie, and Claire Robbins. Although numerous books, articles, and monographs describe class and group exercises, they are often designed primarily for use by instructors or trainers. Our interest, however, is in having you learn to lead, not just participate in, group learning experiences. We encourage you to incorporate the use of group learning processes and strategies for collaborative task accomplishment into your practice. Therefore, in addition to providing you with learning exercises and experiences, the workbook seeks to present these materials in ways that allow you, in turn, to use them in your own work with groups, communities, and organizations.

This workbook is designed for students of community practice and will provide you with opportunities and challenges to take risks in practice in the presence of both your peers and your instructor or trainer. Taking risks, trying out new roles and skills, and helping community members do the same are central aspects of work with communities, groups, and organizations. That is, the workbook is built on parallel processes: what you learn, you will teach and coach others to do.

We hope that the workbook will prove useful to you in developing competence and confidence in community practice skills, and assist you in your ongoing work with groups, organizations, and communities. There are always differences in local circumstances and issues faced by groups and organizations seeking to increase their abilities to shape and improve the direction of their lives and the futures of their communities. Therefore different models of community practice and combinations of approaches will call for emphasis on particular sets of roles and skills that the worker will need to personally employ and in many instances coach residents to master in order to achieve community goals.

In order to emphasize both the essential value of basic processes, such as facilitation and empowerment, and to more deeply explore distinctions of particular skill sets, the workbook is organized into chapters that parallel the text. Early workbook chapters focus on knowledge and values that undergird all community practice, while most of the chapters focus on specific skills and approaches to strengthen your work in each of the eight community practice models that we explore.

We are interested in your ideas and feedback—from students, community practitioners, and faculty—about the workbook and hope that you will communicate with us. There will be opportunities over time to fine-tune and update workbook materials, and we will be very interested in your ideas about ways to increase the usefulness of the workbook through recommendations, critiques, questions, and examples from your own practice. We can be contacted through the School of Social Work at the University of North Carolina, Chapel Hill: Dee Gamble (dng3040@email.unc.edu) and Marie Weil (moweil@email.unc.edu). Please use the subject heading *Community Practice Skills* for any communications.

We hope you will take the information, exercises, and experiences from this workbook and the *Community Practice Skills* text to use in your current and future practice; and we encourage you to adapt and amplify the knowledge and skills gained to teach, coach, and empower the people with whom you work.

Marie Weil, Dee Gamble, and Emily MacGuire

PART I

INTRODUCTORY EXERCISES: INSPIRATION, CHALLENGE, HOPE, RESILIENCE, AND SUSTAINING EFFORTS

As you deepen your study of community practice, it is important to reflect back on how you initially became interested in work with communities and to recognize and acknowledge the person or persons who inspired you to take up the challenge.

The following two exercises tap into our feelings, purposes, commitments, and directions in community practice. Work with communities is undertaken by people with a passion for social justice and a desire to make a positive difference in the lives of people and communities that face social and economic hardship, environmental degradation, and often exclusion from full civic participation. The work engages not only our minds, but our emotions and spirit. Community practice is challenging; we and the people we work with often face barriers, and the needed responses are often complex. Because the work is hard and requires resilience and commitment, we especially need to remember and nourish our inspirations, share vision and inspiration with our colleagues and community groups, and build on the power of hope so that all of us—with support and shared commitment—can sustain our efforts for positive change over the long haul.

SMALL-GROUP EXERCISE: HISTORICAL AND CONTEMPORARY INSPIRATIONS

Modified Nominal Group Technique, about 30 minutes

This exercise and many others in the workbook can be used in experiential learning in class and can equally well be used in your own practice with community groups or organizations.

This first activity can be completed during the first or second class meeting. It engages people in thinking about those who have been an inspiration to them. Members will learn from each other about a broader spectrum of leaders and community work. In a community that you work with, this exercise allows group members to reflect on their own commitment to community change by thinking about earlier leaders. In addition younger people will learn more about neighborhood history, while older participants learn from youth and young adults.

Preparation: The materials you will need include paper and pens, large poster/newsprint paper, large markers, and tape.

Setting: Be sure that the room or meeting area has movable chairs, as both small and larger group arrangements will be used.

Process: The class (or group) should divide themselves into small subgroups so that each group includes a minimum of four people and a maximum of six people. Each small group should choose a facilitator and a reporter. Groups will individually and jointly brainstorm to identify inspirational leaders in community work they know from contemporary experience or from historical knowledge.

Individually make notes about inspirational leaders you wish to present. Each facilitator should then assist her or his group in a "round-robin" listing of the people each member has noted. Each speaker should describe the nominated person's work and his or her contribution to the community.

Small-group reporters will record on poster paper (divided into two columns) the community leaders identified within their group. They may be neighborhood/village leaders or leaders at state or national levels who have provided vision and inspiration. They might be leaders participants know, leaders they learned about from childhood stories, or historical leaders they have learned about through study.

Reporters will list each person's name, where they worked, and the general time period in the first column, and note the focus of their work and contributions, such as community development, social justice, community advocacy, or human rights, in the second column (10 minutes for small groups).

LARGE-GROUP DISCUSSION

Post each subgroup's list and review the people identified by all groups. The class facilitator should lead a discussion to identify leaders who have been named by multiple groups, ask group members to clarify information about persons whom others are not familiar with, and ask the group to add other inspirational figures and information about them.

Summarize by asking the group:

1. To describe what it means to inspire hope.
2. To describe how some of the leaders identified demonstrated resilience in the face of tough challenges.
3. To explain how they showed courage to sustain their efforts over the long haul.
4. To discuss why it is valuable to think about the work and lives of the people identified.

To conclude, the facilitator should weave together and summarize the themes raised by class members. (Ask a class member to take the poster sheets and type up a summary list of the people noted and their work, which will be distributed at the next class.)

GROUP EXERCISE: NAMING AND CLAIMING MENTORS, AND IMPORTANCE OF SYMBOLS

30–40 minutes, depending on size of group

This activity can be completed between the fourth and seventh class meetings. It is more personal, and class or group members may need time to connect with each other and establish trust before speaking out about their personal mentors. *When using this activity with community groups, it will be very important to give people time to get to know each other, and build their shared purpose and commitment to positive change. After several community meetings, you can plan with members of the group how to conduct such an activity, focusing on the contributions of present and past local community leaders.*

Preparation: Two weeks prior to conducting this activity, ask participants to bring something into class on the day of the exercise—an object that symbolizes their interest in and commitment to become community practitioners, or an object that symbolizes an experience that set them on their path for practice. Remind participants the week before to bring their object of interest—and e-mail a final prompt.

Setting: Arrange chairs in a circle. Participants should assemble in a circle—standing or seated—with the object they have brought to class with them. Place a lighted candle or a flower in the center of the circle. This small ceremony denotes the importance of the discussion.

Process: This activity could be conducted in the second, third, or fourth class and most likely should be conducted during the second half of the class session.

DYAD DISCUSSION

The facilitator should ask class members to divide into dyads (and a triad if needed) by selecting a person in the group whom they do not know well. Participants should move into adjacent chairs for their "dyad" discussion so that they can speak comfortably to each other. Each person in turn should tell her or his discussion partner about a person who has been an inspirational mentor. Your "mentor" may be someone you have known very well, someone you have worked with, or someone whose work you have studied or witnessed. Tell your partner why this person has been very important in your life and in thinking about your own life's work. (The dyads should have 6 minutes together.) Then bring the whole group back together and ask them to stand in a circle and place their symbolic object in the chair behind them.

FULL-GROUP CONVENING

The group facilitator or instructor explains that this is an exercise to "name and claim our mentors." All participants, starting with the facilitator (to model the activity), will name and say one or two sentences about their own mentor and why the mentor has been an important influence in their lives. Each person around the circle should speak in turn in a voice that can be heard by the full group.

MEANINGFUL SYMBOLS

When everyone has presented their mentor in this brief round, the facilitator asks the members to remain in the circle and explains that now each person will briefly say why the object that they brought to class has special meaning (or what it symbolizes) to them in relation to their goals and choice of community practice. After asking participants to hold their symbolic object, the facilitator speaks first, then indicates that people will speak in order around the circle, beginning with the person on the facilitator's left.

When everyone has presented their symbolic object, the facilitator should move to the center of the circle and blow out the candle or pick up the flower. Then the facilitator should rejoin the circle and note that sharing these kinds of experiences based on values and feelings is one of the ways that we can assist groups in opening up to each other and building trust. The facilitator may also explain that either the "mentor" exercise or the "symbolic object" exercise may be used separately with groups students will work with.

Thank everyone for their willingness to share thoughts about their mentors and their own goals, and conclude the class. The following week it may be helpful to ask the group about any thoughts prompted by this exercise and the earlier one on historical and contemporary community and community practice leaders.

1

COMMUNITIES AND COMMUNITY PRACTICE IN LOCAL TO GLOBAL CONTEXTS

In the first chapter of *Community Practice Skills (CPS)* we introduce a number of concepts that we develop in greater detail throughout the book. The five exercises in this chapter will help you become familiar with the concepts, allow you to critique the perspectives introduced using concepts you may have already acquired, and challenge you to apply these concepts to your professional development. We encourage you to explore these exercises with your classmates and instructor to see how you might expand or amend them in order to deepen your understanding of the concepts, processes, and ideas we have introduced.

SMALL-GROUP EXERCISE: THE MEANING OF COMMUNITY

Divide up into small groups of three or four. In the *CPS* text refer to the diagram in chapter 1 of "Maureen Hart's Community Capital Triangle" (figure 1.1; also reprinted as figure W7.1 in the workbook). You can also locate the triangle at the Web site: www.sustainablemeasures.com. Consider the local community that you come from or where you currently live. In this case we are referring to a geographic location rather than a community of interest. It may be a village, a small town or city, a neighborhood in a city, a suburb, or a barrio. Rotating turns among group members, take each of Hart's levels of community capital in turn and describe specific elements in your local communities that fit into the different levels: "Natural Capital," "Human and Social Capital," and "Built Capital."

Discuss among yourselves which of the levels contributes most to the well-being of each of your communities:

- Natural Capital, which may include natural resources, ecosystem services (e.g., fertile soil, water filtration, and clean air), and the beauty of nature.
- Human and Social Capital, which may include people, connections with human organizations (e.g., families, neighborhoods), and economic and political institutions.
- Built Capital, which may include methods of communication, equipment, roads, buildings, factories, and hospitals.

For each of your communities, discuss which of the levels is most in need of repair or improvement to provide for the community's well-being and why. Compare your perspectives with those of the other small groups.

ROLE PLAYS: COMMUNITY PRACTICE PROCESSES

In teams of four to six, develop role plays outside of class representing one of the four practice processes and present each group's role play in class. In chapter 1 of the *CPS* textbook, we have described Weil's community practice processes as *organizing, planning, sustainable development,* and *movements for progressive change.* Review the descriptions of these processes in the textbook. Would you recognize these processes if you saw them in action? Test your ability to portray these community practice processes. Each team will take one of the four processes and develop a 15-minute mini-drama or role play that represents the process. Focus your mini-drama around five words or phrases that you might display on a poster during the drama that best represents what you are portraying. After presentation of the four mini-dramas, the entire class will identify the most distinguishing features of each of the four processes as well as aspects that make them similar.

INDIVIDUAL WRITTEN EXERCISE: SOCIAL JUSTICE AND HUMAN RIGHTS IN PROFESSIONAL DEVELOPMENT

Review the discussion in chapter 1 to identify the specific professional anchors for social justice and human rights. Also, review how poverty and the Millennium Development Goals relate to understanding of social justice and human rights. Write a broad, one-sentence definition for each of the following concepts that expresses your understanding of

- social justice
- human rights
- the Millennium Development Goals.

Now, describe how these concepts may or may not be reflected in your professional direction or the job you someday dream of doing. Describe how and where the concepts of *social justice* and *human rights* are (or will be) part of your education and training. Finally, state how you plan to use these concepts in your future practice.

In this first chapter we have introduced the concepts of *social justice* and *human rights*; throughout CPS we expand on the meanings and applications of these terms. When you finish studying the CPS textbook, come back to this exercise and see if your definitions of these concepts and your professional direction have changed in any way.

SMALL-GROUP EXERCISE: SOCIAL, ECONOMIC, POLITICAL, AND ENVIRONMENTAL WELL-BEING

In groups of three or four, discuss the similarities and distinctions among the types of *well-being* listed below. In the CPS textbook different aspects of well-being are defined in the following ways:

- **Social well-being** means all people *have access to the supports and opportunities* provided by social institutions and relationships such as families, neighborhoods, communities, educational institutions, health and cultural organizations, religious organizations, and governmental institutions.
- **Economic well-being** means that all people *have opportunities to achieve* a wide variety of livelihoods and that wages should pay enough to meet a family's needs for shelter, food, health care, and transportation.
- **Political well-being** means that all people *should have freedom to associate, speak, vote, and participate* in the governments that make policy for them.
- **Environmental well-being** means that present generations *must not live beyond the resources in the biosphere and must restore*, to the extent possible, damage to air, water, soil, fisheries, forests, and other species.

INDIVIDUAL AND SMALL-GROUP EXERCISE

Independently describe in a few sentences your own relative well-being in each of these four arenas. For each arena identify several indicators that document the condition of your well-being. Divide up into groups of three or four. Compare your perspectives, as well as the differences in the indicators you identified, with those of other members in your small group.

2

CONCEPTUAL FRAMEWORKS AND MODELS
FOR COMMUNITY PRACTICE

In chapter 2 of the *CPS* textbook, we introduced readers to our revised and updated Eight Models of Community Practice originally published in 1995. The revisions incorporate new content that helps to make the eight models a relevant template for many community groups across the globe. We also focus on three lenses that we believe will influence community practice no matter where one engages with this work during the coming decades: globalization, the increase in multicultural societies, and the expansion of human rights, especially the rights of women and girls. Finally, we introduce the primary and related roles that relate to the eight-model structure. The following exercises are designed to take your understanding of the eight models, the three lenses, and the twenty-one practice roles to a deeper level of understanding and to help you apply these understandings to your professional development.

SMALL-GROUP EXERCISE: APPLYING ISSUES OF DIVERSITY TO THE EIGHT MODELS OF COMMUNITY PRACTICE

Form small groups of two or four. There should be at least one small group for each of the eight models.

Listed here are questions that help community practice workers think and act in ways that will be inclusive. These questions focus on diversity and the application of the full range of diversity considerations to the eight models. Assume your small group is a team of organizers or facilitators who conduct training for that particular model. Discuss how you would respond to the questions, and what specific knowledge and skills you could bring to help an organization or community group be more responsive to women and girls, to people who represent a range of cultures, classes, gender identities, ages, and usually excluded perspectives. We thank Paul Castelloe, Dee Gamble, Marie Weil, and Evelyn Williams for contributing to these questions.

A. *Neighborhood and Community Organization*
   1. What are the best ways to maximize the participation of the full spectrum of gender, cultural, and racial diversity in a neighborhood or community at all levels of organization building?
   2. What strategies are most successful to strengthen leadership capacities among people of color and women who live in the neighborhood, parish, or county?
   3. What are the most effective ways to facilitate the empowerment of culturally diverse groups or lower status groups in the local community?
   4. How can facilitators help organizations incorporate social justice goals in their mission and structure, guiding them toward a more cooperative and supportive role with diverse populations in the community?
   5. What strategies are most useful to help local organizations incorporate the unique strengths, hopes, goals, and needs of people from across the diversity spectrum?

B. *Organizing Functional Communities*
   1. How can alternative programs be developed to serve the unique strengths, hopes, goals, and needs of diverse communities of interest (e.g., people of color, women, people who are physically or mentally challenged, people who are poor, refugees, or any group that is stigmatized or denied rights and participation in society)?
   2. What are the best ways to identify leadership capacities among diverse groups in relation to organizing, planning, development, and change strategies?
   3. How can people from nondominant groups best be supported to organize around specific issues?
   4. What strategies work best to build coalitions among people across race, ethnicity, gender, class, gender identity, language, and other diversity characteristics, in order to build common agendas for social justice?
   5. How can functional communities, especially those most often excluded from decision-making and priority-setting circles, increase accountability for social and economic justice in both political and service systems?

C. *Social, Economic, and Sustainable Development*
   1. What are the best ways to identify and acknowledge the social, economic, and environmental contributions of people of color, women, and those living in poverty to the development of any community,

especially those invisible fruits of labor that historically have often benefited only the dominant groups in society?

2. What principles of development will take into account the cultures, strengths, values, and needs of diverse groups of people in any region?

3. How can differences in cultural competence on the part of facilitators affect the outcomes for any community in successfully developing sustainable livelihoods and viable economic opportunities?

4. What are the best ways to develop and support the inclusion of a wide diversity of people from any region in the full participation of development planning, including goal setting, implementation, governance, and evaluation?

5. How can programs ensure the inclusion of people from diverse racial, ethnic, and economic backgrounds at all levels of development activities?

D. *Inclusive Program Development*

1. How can we ensure that the perspectives of diverse populations are considered in the development of service networks and systems for service coordination?

2. What are the most successful strategies to broaden service program development foci to include the needs of people of color, women, and the elderly—particularly relating to physical health, mental health, or the disabling conditions of poverty and oppression?

3. How can collaborative activities be strengthened between mainstream service systems and alternative programs developed by African Americans, Latinos, Native groups, LGBT groups, or other diverse groups in the community?

4. How can service programs focus on empowerment of and advocacy for oppressed groups?

5. How can service programs develop closer, functional ties to constituent groups and populations involved in services—sharing information, sharing evaluation responsibilities, and co-creating effective services that meet community needs?

6. What are the best strategies to involve constituent groups and service participants in governance and evaluation of programs?

E. *Social Planning*

1. What kinds of policies, programs, and activities give normally excluded groups a chance to develop technical, management, and evaluation skills?

2. What strategies will ensure the involvement of diverse groups from the region in planning, organizing, and developing regional social programs?

3. How can we ensure that planning approaches are grounded in the experiences and aspirations of the target population?

4. What are effective ways to validate the perspectives of people from diverse groups concerning appraisal of the needs and strengths of the community?

5. What structures will ensure the democratization of planning processes, especially regarding issues of cultural diversity and gender identity?

6. How can the planning processes be demystified? How can technical skills and analysis methods be adapted appropriately in relation to local culture and technology?

7. In what ways can we intentionally use theory, values, principles, and perspectives developed within groups related to cultural diversity (e.g., Afrocentric, Indian and indigenous perspectives, Latino–recent immigrant, Latino–here before the Europeans, women-centered, pro-poor, etc.) in social planning?

F. *Coalitions*

1. How can organizations and community workers help develop coalitions that concern themselves with the social and economic empowerment of people most often excluded from such opportunities?

2. How can programs initiated by people representing diverse experiences form coalitions that will strengthen service networks?

3. How can groups formed by people representing diverse experiences and backgrounds be assisted to find common ground?

4. What are the best ways to work with coalitions so that they can deal with the inherent tensions caused by centripetal (moving toward the group) and centrifugal (moving away from the group) forces that can either strengthen individuals' investment in the coalition's work or weaken connections to the coalition because of work pressures or demands at their "home organization"?

5. How can coalitions be formed with the dominant groups that work to eliminate racism and poverty in society?

G. *Political and Social Action*

1. How can the power of traditionally excluded groups of people be increased to influence policy decisions?

2. What are the best ways to maximize the participation of people from diverse perspectives in political systems and institutions?

3. What activities will strengthen morale and build the skills of people most often excluded from participation in political and advocacy groups?

4. How can we achieve the full representation of diverse population groups in existing political structures?

    5. What strategies successfully include diverse groups of people in social and political decision-making processes with the goal of developing continued collective power?

  H. *Movements for Progressive Change*

    1. How can grassroots groups, representatives from nongovernmental organizations and community-based organizations, grantmakers, and academics best be engaged in emerging movements that focus on improving the quality of life for all people no matter what their cultural heritage, such as sustainable development, human development, and the movement for the rights of children?

    2. What are the best strategies to engage women and men from all cultures and ethnic groups in the movements to eliminate all forms of violence against women and eliminate state-supported violence?

    3. How can social movements support opportunities for people from a wide range of cultural perspectives to participate?

If there is time following the small-group exercise, the small groups can share their insights and strategy proposals with the whole group.

INDIVIDUAL EXERCISE/CLASS PRESENTATION: LENSES INFLUENCING COMMUNITY PRACTICE IN THIS CENTURY

In this chapter in *CPS* we describe three "lenses" that will affect community practice in this century almost anywhere in the world. These lenses are

- Globalization
- The Increase in Multicultural Societies
- The Expansion of Human Rights, Especially for Women and Girls

Read the descriptions of these three lenses in the *CPS* textbook. You might also explore a number of Web sites that can give globalization, multicultural societies, and expansion of human rights broader meaning. For example, this NOVA Web site compares the relative material wealth of families around the globe: http://www.pbs.org/wgbh/nova/worldbalance/material.html. A video clip that can help you explore human rights issues is Unnatural Causes 3rd segment: http://www.unnaturalcauses.org/video_clips.php.

    The Association for Women's Rights in Development (AWID) Web site can also provide some insight into the lenses we have identified: http://www.awid .org/. The Organization for Economic Co-operation and Development (OECD) has also developed a formula for measuring gender equality by calculating the root causes of inequalities. You can find the Social Institutions and Gender Index by searching the Web site for OECD SIGI.

Find newspaper articles (hard copy or an online news source that is widely read in your area) from the last month that have a focus on one or more of the lenses. Bring the articles to class and be prepared to present your critical assessment describing:

- How the article applies to the particular lens you have identified. In your presentation describe the particular progressive or positive aspects as well as the challenges or negative aspects your news articles open up in relation to the lens you have identified.
- How the lens you have identified could influence community practice work you would like to do in the future.

INDIVIDUAL ACTIVITY: PRIMARY AND RELATED ROLES ASSOCIATED WITH THE EIGHT MODELS

Review the definitions of the primary and related roles identified in table 2.2 of the *CPS* textbook. Selecting from both primary and related roles, list those you believe would best suit your personality and skills, with notes that justify your selections. Then, develop a second list of roles in which you would like to become more skilled, again with notes to explain why you would like to increase your skills and how you will work to increase skills for that role.

Discuss your selections with peers and mentors to explore and affirm your choices. Ask them for suggestions for how you might strengthen your skills and where you could get experiences to practice skills you would like to further develop.

3

EVOLUTION OF VALUES, CONCEPTS,
AND COMMUNITY PRACTICE APPROACHES

INDIVIDUAL ACTIVITY: VALUES AND VALUE CLARIFICATION—PERSONAL REFLECTION PAPER

This activity is to be prepared for your own clarification and use—not to be turned in for class. However, bring a copy to class so that you can discuss items that you are comfortable sharing with your colleagues and instructor.

Write a statement about where you derive your personal values. Do they come from a humanistic, cultural, and/or religious tradition, or elsewhere? Write a list of your six to seven most deeply held personal values and a paragraph about why they are of special importance to you.

Review the NASW Code of Ethics (or your own national code) and the IFSW/IASSW Statement of Principles from chapter 3 of the *CPS* text. Select and write separate lists including the values/principles/ethical standards from each code that are most important and valuable to you with a paragraph that states why. Then respond to either section A or B below:

A. Are there any points in either professional code/statement that you find hard to identify with, that you disagree with, or that you reject? If so: (1) Write individual statements about your response to each one that poses a problem or concern for you. (2) Conclude your reflection paper with a one-page analysis of this value discrepancy between personally held values and professionally expected principles and values. (3) How do you view these differences? (4) How will you accommodate the differences given the fact that the professional expectation is that you will uphold the social work code of ethics of your national association? (5) What are your current thoughts about how you might resolve conflicts between your personally held and your professionally expected values and ethics? (6) Select points from your analysis that you are comfortable sharing in class discussion about personal and professional values and values clarification and be prepared to discuss those issues.

B. If you experience no conflicts between your personally held values compared to the professional code of your own nation and the IFSW/IASSW Statement of Principles:

(1) Summarize the similarities between the Code and the international groups' Statement of Principles. (2) State which aspects of the ethical code are most meaningful and valuable to you. (3) Analyze the differences between the two codes that are most interesting to you and write your response to what these differences between international principles and national code mean as ideas—that is, philosophically. (4) Explain the implications of the differences for actual professional practice. (5) Select comparison points you are comfortable sharing for a class discussion about personal and professional values and values clarification.

GROUP ACTIVITY: VALUES AND VALUES CLARIFICATION

- First, in small groups of four discuss the points from your reflection paper that you have selected.
- Then discuss selected commonalities and differences with the entire class. Be mindful that, depending on our unique backgrounds and experiences, even groups of community practitioners will have value differences—some of which may be surprising or confusing.
- Part of a values clarification process is to be sure that you actively listen to the ideas and value concerns of others. Establish group norms that no one is to be interrupted while they briefly present their own value concerns. Also include a group norm that even if you deeply disagree with someone else's viewpoint, it is important to learn to understand their position. As part of the exercise it is fine to ask questions for clarification; it is not okay to attack someone else's value position. There will be time for issue debates later in the course. Skillful facilitation is an essential aspect of positively focused values clarification exercises; and such discussions should be handled so that all are encouraged to think carefully about values and that no one in the group should feel attacked.
- After your class discussion of value perspectives, as a group select issues and concerns that you will want to discuss later in class in relation to actual practice and/or case examples.
- For further discussion, bear in mind that throughout your work in community practice you will encounter individuals and groups (in communities,

in related organizations and governmental programs or positions) that disagree—sometimes vehemently—with your own position or that of your group. In this exercise there is no expectation that you will change your own value perspectives, only that you will have a deeper understanding of your own values, a recognition that others may not agree with some of your values, and that you will work to understand the values held by others.

- However, as students proceed through professional education and development, it is not unusual to find that you experience some value shifts or modifications as you gain more experience and work with diverse groups, communities, and organizations.
- An important aspect of professional education is to reexamine ethical codes and the IFSW/IASSW principles when value issues arise in practice. After careful study of these documents, and the values clarification work in class, give further consideration to the degree of congruity between your personal values and the professionally expected values and principles. If you find yourself in stark disagreement on essential issues—such as equal human rights, principles and action for social justice, and the need to actively respond to the needs of the poor and dispossessed—it will be important for you to give thoughtful consideration to your professional goals.

Social work and community practice are historically and ethically grounded in concern for human rights and the promotion of social justice. If you do not share these concerns, you should seriously consider moving closer to a career that embodies your own values. There are other vocations and professions which may be more compatible with your value perspective. Authenticity and professional integrity are critical factors in your relations and work with groups and communities. In practice you are likely to be asked your positions on some hotly debated issues related to essential values. The class may wish to discuss such concerns and professional integrity in more detail in later sessions.

INDIVIDUAL ACTIVITY AND CLASS DISCUSSION: EXPLORING CULTURES, VALUES, AND RELIGIOUS PHILOSOPHIES

INDIVIDUAL OR SMALL-GROUP ACTIVITY

Select one of the philosophies of religion/value perspective that is not of your own tradition (or that of your family) and visit a service or gathering at a place that practices that tradition. If your perspective is primarily humanistic, you might choose to visit a meeting of a local Society for Ethical Culture or another organization or activist group that is grounded in humanist values.

Depending on what opportunities are available in your area, two or three class members might want to make a visit together. It would be useful for class discussion if your class members are able to cover the major traditions discussed in the chapter. If you are unable to visit, read about the tradition and write a reflection paper comparing and contrasting the commonalities and differences between that philosophy and your own. There are numerous Web sites for reference material in this area—both specific traditions and philosophies and comparative treatments. Following your visits or Web explorations, engage in a class discussion to compare and contrast each of the discussed traditions.

VIDEO: VALUES IN CONFLICT

As a class, watch "A Walk to Beautiful," a PBS program about the global issue of fistula: http://www.pbs.org/wgbh/nova/beautiful/.

DISCUSSION QUESTIONS ABOUT THE VIDEO: (1) Share your thoughts and discuss everyone's reactions to the film. (2) Examine the differences between "universal values" and "relative values." (3) Individually, where do you stand on the expectation (a) that specific cultural values (relative values) should be respected and maintained because they are part of a people's tradition/culture/religion; or (b) that basic, universal human rights should be respected and promoted over a culturally entrenched value/practice that is discriminatory, demeaning, or oppressive to some groups—although the practice is accepted in some societies.

Divide the class into two groups, one generally in agreement with position (a) and one generally in agreement with position (b). Take 10 minutes for each group to write on newsprint or easel paper their strongest arguments to defend the position that they are taking in class. Then take 5 minutes each for the two groups to present their position. Conclude with a general discussion about how professionals, NGOs, and international organizations should relate to these value questions and the actual experiences of the women portrayed in "A Walk to Beautiful." If time allows, identify and discuss additional issues that pose the tension between culturally based relative values and claims for basic human values.

CLASS DISCUSSIONS AND INDIVIDUAL HOMEWORK ACTIVITY

CLASS DISCUSSION

Jim Ife, a noted Australian human rights scholar and activist, has identified the following seven categories of human rights he believes should exist for all people: social; civic and political; economic; cultural; gender; environmental; personal/ spiritual.

In class discussion develop your group definition of each of the rights areas. The instructor or a class member should copy the definitions you develop as a group and make them available to all class members.

INDIVIDUAL HOMEWORK ASSIGNMENT

Ife's categories are illustrated in table W3.1. You are asked to complete the individual homework activity presented in the table.

CLASS DISCUSSION

In your next class discuss members' ideas and findings about the status of human rights in diverse nations as documented in your individual responses to the questions and comparisons in table W3.1.

CLASS DISCUSSION

- Compare and contrast the class's responses regarding culturally relative values/rights and universal values/rights in relation to "A Walk to Beautiful" with class responses to Ife's position on human rights and class members' perspectives and findings in response to the questions raised in table W3.1.
- What conclusions do you draw about the current comparative state of human rights?

QUESTIONS TO DISCUSS IN CLASS

- Have you personally seen anyone's human rights violated? Please share examples with the class.

TABLE W3.1 Ife's Categories of Human Rights

SOCIAL	CIVIC & POLITICAL	ECONOMIC	CULTURAL	GENDER	ENVIRONMENTAL	PERSONAL/ SPIRITUAL

In work done out of class, select four of Ife's categories and write a brief comparative analysis in which you (1) identify the four areas you will discuss; (2) add the class's definition or your own definition of the four types of rights; (3) select two nations (your own and another that you are familiar with) and compare and describe the current status of each of the four rights areas in each of the two nations:

STATUS OF RIGHTS IN TWO NATIONS

Selection of Four Categories of Rights to Compare	Nation 1 Current Status of Rights	Nation 2 Current Status of Rights

Respond to the following questions about the rights you have selected in both nations:

(a) How is each right actively expressed in each nation?

Specific Rights Area	Nation 1	Nation 2

(b) Are rights the same and equal for everyone?

Specific Rights Area	Nation 1	Nation 2

(*continued*)

TABLE W3.1 (*continued*)

(c) Are any groups excluded? If so, on what basis?

Specific Rights Area	Nation 1	Nation 2

(d) Are there rights in either nation that need legislative protection?

Specific Rights Area	Nation 1	Nation 2

- Have you experienced a violation of basic rights yourself? If comfortable, please share with class.
- How do you know specific rights freely exist in cultures you have lived and worked in?
- Select a specific right—such as free speech—to discuss with regard to how this "right" may be defined differently in different countries.

CLASS DISCUSSION: CULTURE, VALUES, AND SOCIAL JUSTICE

Visit the following Web site to review the "Cultural View Finder," which offers excellent cultural questions related to needs, social habits, religion, politics, economics, technology, and environment: http://gdnhome.com/viewfinder/needs. html. Consider your own history and how your culture relates to questions that are brought up on the site. Discuss your reactions to the information on the Web site in relation to different cultures, different values, and your own perspectives on social justice.

4

THEORIES AND PERSPECTIVES
FOR COMMUNITY PRACTICE

This chapter involves you in examining and applying theories and perspectives that relate to and can guide different aspects of community practice. We also invite you to engage in practicing "theorizing" and encourage you to consider incorporating the processes of theorizing and of applying (testing) your ideas as an essential component of your own practice. Practice should not consist of one random action after another in hopes of achieving a goal. Rather, practice should be guided by theories, research evidence, and identified best practices. Through examining and comparing processes of work and outcomes from different projects and programs, we can develop more effective (and reliable) approaches to practice that can in fact more often lead to successful outcomes in group, organizational, and community endeavors.

Reread the case example about Jane Addams that opens chapter 4 in *Community Practice Skills*. This brief excerpt from *Twenty Years at Hull-House* about the development of the settlement's coffee café illustrates a moment of enlightenment for Addams as she learned to deeply listen to community members—adolescents and adults from many ethnic immigrant groups—who participated in Hull-House programs and activities.

What Addams realized is that community members themselves can best tell us what they need and want to improve the quality of their lives—and life in their communities. Hull-House staff had been debating for a considerable time regarding the kind of food they should serve in their new facility. Initially they relied on the expert advice of nutritionists regarding what the neighborhood people should eat. The staff's first approach to serving food was met with considerable disapproval—and indeed rebuff from community members—because the "nutritious food" being served seemed to the immigrant populations in the neighborhood, especially those from Mediterranean countries and Eastern Europe, to be hopelessly bland and tasteless. In addition, for quite some time, Addams and other Hull-House staff had ignored community members' requests that a food venue be a "coffee café"—such as one might find in many parts of Europe—a comfortable space, with good coffees and teas, and a menu of different foods that "tasted more like home." The staff wanted to provide a place that was "unlike the local saloons," but they did not initially stop to learn what members of the community longed for in a food venue.

Aside from experiencing a powerful moment of realization, Addams used the opportunity to "theorize" before taking action. That is, she considered the meanings of what had occurred and derived some theoretical principles that we would now label essential components of empowerment theory. Addams realized that much of what she and other settlement workers needed to know to build successful programs and influence policies would "come from the people." She took to heart, in a new way, ideas about promoting choice and decision making within and among groups. As we might say now, she recognized that "people are the experts about their own lives and their own communities"; and that in order to work effectively to improve well-being and increase opportunities in communities, we must first *listen to and learn from the groups that we hope to serve and empower.* Being open to such realizations, developing principles that express ways we should work and interact, and then working to create and test our own theories of action are all components of compassionate and competent community practice.

INDIVIDUAL ACTIVITY: THEORIZING

- To move in this needed direction for empowerment, reflect on your own experiences in community practice or other "real case" scenarios.
- Review Beth Reed's theory chart in *CPS*, chapter 4, and again give consideration to her explanation of *theorizing*; also review the "Framework for Community Practice Theory" in table 4.3 of *CPS*, chapter 4, and consider which theories you would be interested in applying to your own experience or the case example you have selected.
- Select a particular real-life practice situation, issue, or problem related to your work (or a recommended case example) with groups, communities, and organizations. Choose a situation in which there are problems that you are unsure how to handle.
- Then *practice theorizing.* Analyze your practice situation and the questions you have about next steps. Identify the theories in Reed's chart that you think will be helpful for problem solving in your practice situation.
- Determine the questions you need to ask yourself and others to get a better "fix" on the issue. Select ideas, approaches, and theories from either or both charts to think through/theorize about the problem to be solved. Construct a

list of the components of your own theory of action. What strategies and actions do the theories recommend or point toward that would be most applicable to solve the practice situation of concern to you? Review and logically organize the ideas you have generated that emerge from your theorizing about the practice situation. Note the points you are using from the theory and write down your new *working theory* or *theory of action.* Finally, explain your new theory of action and why you think it will have the intended effect on your practice situation. Is there research that might confirm your theory? If not, what research and experience would confirm its usefulness? What positive change would you expect to see if your actions based on the working theory effectively deal with the concern? That is, "What would success look like?" If possible, test out your theory of action in practice and document the results.

Given the situation you are working on, consider which of the following options—or an option of your own creation—is most likely to fit your practice situation:

- If you have constructed a theory of action that focuses on how you work with groups or members of organizations or communities, test out your working theory in discussion with colleagues and solicit their critiques and recommendations. Refine your "theory of action" and test it out in practice.
- If you have constructed a theory of action that focuses on how different groups might work better together, go through the same process just described, and after consulting with colleagues, convert your "working theory" into an action plan and involve members of the groups you are working with in discussing and assessing the approach. Then test out the revised action plan.

You may find that one or two theoretical approaches seem most applicable and promising for the given situation. Make notes on your own "thinking-through/theorizing" process and be prepared to share some of your thoughts with class members in a discussion about theorizing, constructing theories, and the use of theories.

Write down your conclusions from this process and test out how your theory of action works in the real world.

SMALL-GROUP DISCUSSION AND PLAN: EMPOWERMENT THEORY AND THEORIZING

In small groups of four or five people, review your knowledge about empowerment theory. Have a group reporter write down on easel paper the major points, principles, and ideas the group shares about this theory and its uses.

Then construct a brief scenario about a practice task group (real for one or more of you, or an imagined group) in which members are stymied about what to do next about a new community or organizational issue, a concern, or an internal or external problem (your class group should select and write a brief description of the issue). As a whole class, identify and apply material available in the workbook or *CPS* text or from other previous readings that may help to bring a productive conclusion to the practice group situation.

Using your knowledge of empowerment approaches and theory, develop a plan and strategy to help the selected practice group (real or hypothetical) rekindle energy for joint work, regenerate ideas, theorize, and develop their own strategies for action.

Using bullet points, the "reporter" will write down the steps in your class group's plan and your strategy for action. Highlight where and how you are using ideas and principles related to empowerment theory.

After 35 to 40 minutes of group deliberation and planning, each class subgroup will share their process of theorizing and their ideas for strategy and action with the whole class.

SMALL-GROUP DISCUSSION AND ROLE PLAY: SOCIAL CAPITAL

- As a large group, construct two community scenarios in which students have or might have responsibilities for facilitating discussions or training.
- One scenario should relate to coaching community group members about ways of developing and using "bonding social capital"—for themselves and their community projects. The other scenario should focus on coaching/ training community group members about "bridging social capital" and how to use it to strengthen their community projects.
- Depending on class size, divide into two groups—one "bonding social capital group" and one "bridging social capital group"—or into four groups with two "bonding" and two "bridging" groups.
- The task is to develop a role play in which each small group focuses on a particular aspect of coaching and discussion about building and using either bonding social capital or bridging social capital to assist community members, support economic development, or assist in another community change process.
- Each role play should model the work of a facilitative leader that is both clear and transparent in coaching and teaching about the selected aspect of social capital.

Allow 20 minutes for small groups to plan and 20 minutes to demonstrate the role plays. After the role plays have been presented, discuss with the full class both the processes and tasks each group is recommending to facilitate understanding and application of "bonding" or "bridging" social capital and the processes your groups used to make decisions about how to employ these concepts in coaching or training.

INDIVIDUAL REFLECTION PAPER: DEVELOPING THEORETICAL UNDERSTANDING

For your next class, write a brief (three-page) reflection paper that will help deepen your understanding of theories that may be complementary and assist you in working with groups and communities at multiple levels.

Select one theory from table 4.3 in chapter 4 of the *CPS* text that is of interest to you. In your paper, briefly describe the scope, purpose, and possible applications of the theory to a specific level of intervention. Then think about a practice situation in which you would be developing a program or project (with goals and outcomes) that would involve you in work at multiple intervention levels—interpersonal; group; organizational and interorganizational; and community. Figure out what additional theories at the four levels you would need to apply in order to work effectively at each intervention to accomplish the goals related to the project or program.

For example, to develop a community-based program to build social capital you might employ the following theories from different intervention levels: *interpersonal* communication theory, *group* theory, and *collaboration* theory with multiple, diverse community groups in order to study, document, and work to expand bonding and bridging social capital in that community. In your paper, state the purpose and the way you would apply at least one theory at interpersonal, group, organizational and interorganizational, and community levels to achieve the goals of your program or project.

CLASS DISCUSSION

In class discuss the approaches members took in using theory at each intervention level, and through dialogue see if class members can come to a consensus about salient points to guide use of theory in community practice at each of the levels of intervention.

PART II

Part II of the *CPS* workbook introduces the community practice student to a wide range of exercises relevant for each of the eight models of community practice in our framework. As we noted in the beginning, these exercises are intended to deepen your knowledge and skill sets for community practice work. We encourage you to modify any of the suggested exercises that will help you expand your understanding and ability to help others in their struggles for social justice and human rights. We also encourage you to modify the exercises so that they will more closely reflect the cultural and historical context of your own practice, as well as reflect the range of diversity existing in the local, regional, or global reach of your work.

5

NEIGHBORHOOD AND COMMUNITY ORGANIZING

The skills needed for neighborhood and community organizing work are basic to all of community practice. This model of community practice focuses on a geographically circumscribed area, and the primary skills relate to how to help people in groups form and develop strong organizations that will allow them to accomplish their goals. Both products and processes will be important in effective neighborhood and community organizing. Face-to-face communication and decision making, as well as valuing and defining a sense of place, become constant and evolving activities in neighborhood and community organizing.

In chapter 5 of the *CPS* textbook we refer to two case examples. One is included at the end of chapter 5—"South African Community Work in Practice: Langa KwaNobuhle Self-Help and Resource Exchange." The other—"Farmer-to-Farmer Integrated Rural Development for Smallholders in Guatemala: Organization in the Face of Natural Disaster and Civil Conflict"—is presented here. It may be helpful to read through the two case studies now so that you can envision how neighborhood and community organizing might work and so that you are prepared to respond to the discussion questions at the end of this section. The South African case example describes the efforts to organize African ethnic groups who had been forcibly removed from their urban neighborhood by the white apartheid government. The second case example describes indigenous rural Guatemalans organizing to improve their economic, social, and health conditions. Discussion questions relating to the roles and skills of the organizers will follow.

FARMER-TO-FARMER INTEGRATED RURAL DEVELOPMENT FOR SMALLHOLDERS IN GUATEMALA: ORGANIZATION IN THE FACE OF NATURAL DISASTER AND CIVIL CONFLICT

ANIRUDH KRISHNA WITH ROLAND BUNCH

The San Martin farmer-to-farmer program officially functioned between 1972 and 1979 with assistance from World Neighbors organizers/technical assistants and funding from Oxfam America. It continued to make progress in crop yields without external assistance even after an earthquake in 1976 and brutal civil conflict that disrupted many villages and lasted from 1978 to 1985. It is located within the department of Chimaltenango in the central highlands of Guatemala. Most of the approximately 60,000 people who live in the San Martin Jilotepeque region are Cakchiquel Indians.

In the decade before the project began, a young Kansas physician, Carroll Behrhorst, opened a clinic sponsored by the Lutheran Church. The medical problems he encountered were often caused or exacerbated by malnutrition and protein deficiency. The local economy was agrarian, however the soils were too eroded, washed away by the rains, and the soil fertility was too low because of continuous cropping. Behrhorst asked World Neighbors, a small international development program, to assist in developing a health and agricultural program.

With a small grant Behrhorst began to train lay health promoters. A team of three World Neighbors agriculturalists and teachers and three local agricultural promoters began work with forty-six communities in Chimaltenango in an effort to address health, nutrition, veterinary medicine, fruit and vegetable production, soil conservation ditches, and terracing. The team soon learned they were trying to do much too much, and scaled back to focus just on the smaller geographic area of San Martin.

Oxfam was also interested in contributing to the organizational effort and supported the integrated development approach. World Neighbors' goal was that local people could take over the program within two years.

While some people suggested the San Martin farmers would never abandon their old ways of farming, others saw that the earlier project effort in Chimaltenango had stimulated interest among San Martin leadership. Hundreds of people had heard about the program and learned some things from both the successes and failures of that program. Oxfam committed $104,000 for a five-year program with the long-term goals of agricultural development, human development, health and family welfare, and road construction. Actual benefits to the people were to be specific measures in increased agricultural production and a significant decrease in child mortality. Oxfam funds would pay for the organizers' and promoters' salaries (a team of two full-time and six part-time organizers/extensionists), equipment, and operating expenditures for five years. Only one of the full-time staff was a non-Guatemalan World Neighbors employee, Roland Bunch. The local farmers themselves would pay for all the interventions for changes in agricultural practices. Behrhorst and his staff at the clinic would train volunteer health promoters.

The agricultural team started by doing a baseline survey of 600 area families to record crop production levels and family welfare. The survey included building understanding of the local knowledge people had about their soils and agricultural practices. In order to start where people were and build upon their local knowledge, the project

CONTINUED

organizers took local farmers to visit farmers who had already made changes in terracing and uphill conservation ditches to see the difference in soil conditions and crop growth potential.

In the education and coaching phase of the work Bunch had already learned a number of important concepts:

- "Start with what people already know and build upon their knowledge incrementally."
- "Teaching a few ideas to hundreds of people is more effective than teaching hundreds of ideas to one person."
- Teaching hundreds of people provides a "critical mass" so that they could "contribute more to community solidarity and to overall social justice."
- "Teach people only such techniques as they can implement with equipment that they already own or can easily afford."

The primary problems that had to be solved for increased production were the prevention of erosion and the addition of nitrogen and phosphorus to the soil. In the facilitation of discussion for solutions it was important to incorporate "local knowledge, cultural preferences, local skills, and economic conditions" with prevailing technical knowledge of soil types, climate, and agricultural science. The village leaders chose a system of contour ditches, dug every ten to twenty meters, with a planting of high-protein, drought-resistant forage grasses along the upper edges. The grasses trapped eroding soil, leading over time to the buildup of natural terraces. For soil nutrients the Cakchiquel leaders chose chemical fertilizers. At the time not as much was known about green manure cover crops, and the dependence on an external supply of fertilizer was weighed against the malnutrition suffered by their families. (Note: Today Bunch is a promoter of green manure cover crops and no-till agriculture through the organization COSECHA in Tegucigalpa, Honduras.)

The team devised a three-step process to multiply their efforts during the first year:

- Forty local volunteer promoters, respected village leaders who had previously shown willingness to work for their communities, were trained in the new terracing and contour ditch techniques.
- The trained farmers undertook small-scale experimentation and field trials with the new techniques on their own farms.
- Extension work was undertaken by 27 of the original trained volunteers (promoters) so that as a result of their efforts 450 farmers had built contour ditches on their land by the end of the first year.

Given the success of the first year, promoters were able to introduce more ideas such as building compost heaps, having their soil tested, controlling insects, planting narrower rows, vaccinating their animals, experimenting with new crops, and most importantly, crop rotation. As crop production increased in the third year, more than 300 women, organized in small groups, were attending classes on nutrition, parenthood, hygiene, latrine construction, and vegetable gardening. Women also initiated literacy classes and clean drinking water projects.

CONTINUED

The earthquake that rocked Guatemala in 1976 killed 2,900 people (8 percent of the population) in the San Martin *municipio*. That year the agricultural project was suspended and both paid and volunteer staff in the program used all their time to help families learn how to construct earthquake-proof dwellings.

Over time farmers resumed the new practices and, although costs for any new innovations were kept low, a credit cooperative was established to help farmers buy resources such as chemical fertilizer. The co-op was called Kato-ki, meaning "self-help" in Cakchiquel. It was also beginning to serve as a lending source to help landless farmers purchase small farms. The cooperative had nearly 1,000 members by the late 1970s before the civil war reached its zenith.

When civil war erupted it was brutal. In one three-day period in 1982, thirteen villages in the *municipio* of San Martin were temporarily wiped off the map. Between 3,000 and 4,000 people fled to the mountains, surviving on herbs and tree bark for nearly three years before they felt safe enough to return. Efforts made after the war to reestablish the cooperative have not succeeded. However, the productive and innovative spirit of farm families that were part of the agricultural program, and survived the civil conflict, continues.

From the beginning local people played a primary role in the planning, organization, and management of the project. World Neighbors staff provided information/skill training and motivation. The training was built upon experimentation and early, visible successes. Evident success is a powerful motivating force for people who had been taught that their lives were useless. The spirit of the agricultural team was kept high by the many successes in their work (increased participation of farmers, higher yields, new products and new opportunities for farmers, and decreased child mortality) and by using consensus for the majority of decisions. Occasional retreats led by external group dynamics facilitators helped deal with inevitable complaints and residual resentments that build up in any organizational effort.

Two organizing issues challenged the community workers in this project. One was how best to involve women and the other was how to mitigate the ethnic tension and the subsequent ethnic violence. Bunch's perspective is that women in Central America tend not to be involved in agricultural work by cultural tradition. "They don't need any more work than they already have." In San Martin if they had been involved in agriculture it might have been around perennial home gardens and small-scale water management, areas in which they have a real interest. "Agricultural programs should be designed from the start with activities that women want to learn about, and [organizers] should not expect women to integrate themselves into activities (*and* additional work) they don't want to do."

The second challenge related to the limited effect the local community organization could have on national ethnic tensions. Perhaps more work to build bridges between the majority Indian population and the minority Latino population in San Martin might have had some impact on the amelioration of the intensity of the local conflict. In the end ethnic violence temporarily disrupted this effective community effort. The spread of the agricultural successes was much slower following the loss of the Kato-ki cooperative.

Excerpted from A. Krishna, N. Uphoff, and M. J. Esman, eds. (1997), Reasons for Hope: Instructive Experiences in Rural Development, pp. 137–152 (West Hartford, CT: Kumarian Press). Used with permission of the authors and editors.

CONTINUED

Also by Anirudh Krishna: 2002. *Active Social Capital: Tracing the Roots of Democracy and Development.* New York: Columbia University Press.

Also by Roland Bunch: 1982. *Two Ears of Corn: A Guide to People Centered Agricultural Development.* Oklahoma City, OK: World Neighbors.

INDIVIDUAL ANALYSIS AND SMALL-GROUP DISCUSSION: CULTURAL SENSITIVITY, APPROPRIATE ROLES, AND VALUE GUIDES

After reading both case examples, make notes on the following questions and prepare to discuss your responses within a small group:

1. In the Eight Models of Community Practice table in the *CPS* text (table 2.1), we suggest that the primary roles for neighborhood and community organizing are the following: organizer, facilitator, educator, coach, trainer, and bridge-builder (role definitions are presented in table 2.2 of *CPS*).
   - Which roles were used most effectively by the World Neighbors staff in Guatemala and by Ms. Gogo in South Africa?
   - Why were these roles particularly effective?
   - Are different roles needed in rural and urban settings?
   - Could other roles have been employed equally effectively to stimulate participation and move toward social justice outcomes?
2. Imagine yourself in these two settings. List the value base that would guide your work in these two settings to help participants develop solutions to problematic neighborhood/community conditions. List the skills you would need to help the communities reach their goals. Be as specific about values and skills as you can.
3. Discuss your responses to these questions in small groups in your class.

FIELD EXERCISE: OBSERVING AND/OR INTERVIEWING A SKILLED ORGANIZER

Locate a community organization in your own community and set up a field trip, either to engage in a dialogue with the community organizer(s) about how they work and/or to watch them in action at a community or neighborhood meeting. Students might visit individually or in pairs in order not to overwhelm the organizer or the community. Be sure to ask the organizer for good examples about how they work in order to facilitate the development of leadership rather than step into the leadership roles themselves. Also, ask them what values anchor their work. When everyone has made a field trip, discuss your findings and perceptions in class.

INDIVIDUAL ANALYSIS AND SMALL-GROUP DISCUSSION: CULTURALLY SENSITIVE ENGAGEMENT

Being culturally sensitive as you enter a community to facilitate organizational development and work toward community goals is part of a very important skill set. Perhaps you are lucky enough to be able to spend time helping a community to organize and reach their goals. If not, imagine a community you would really like to help get organized.

Write answers for yourself to the "Who, How, and What" questions described below in preparation for work with either the real community or the hypothetical community with whom you would like to engage. After you have written answers for yourself, meet with at least three or four other students who have done the same. Compare your answers. Describe the parts of engagement you think will be most difficult. Describe the things you have learned about yourself in this discussion that will make you an effective, culturally sensitive organizer/facilitator.

THE "WHO, HOW, AND WHAT" QUESTIONS

ADAPTED FROM CHRISTINE ROBINSON, "THE WHO QUESTIONS" (UNPUBLISHED PAPER, SCHOOL OF SOCIAL WORK, UNIVERSITY OF NORTH CAROLINA, 1996)

- Who am I? How do I describe myself physically, in terms of my beliefs, motivations, expectations, fears, cultural values, religious beliefs and tolerance, and gender expectations?
- Who are the people in this community? What is my knowledge of their beliefs, motivations, expectations, fears, and cultural values? Are there people in the community I might find harder to reach? Do I have a strategy for getting to know the range of diverse people who live in the community?
- How will the community view me? What previous experience does this community have with organizers? How will the community members regard my age, sex, sexual orientation, language, education, dress, and religion or lack of religion?
- What are my best competencies (integrated knowledge, judgment, and skills) for joining in a partnership with members of this community to promote improved social, economic, and environmental conditions?

IN-CLASS FISHBOWL EXERCISE: FACILITATION AND DIALOGUE

Helping people to talk with each other, to be able to hear what they are saying to each other while not taking over the framing of issues, requires particular skills in facilitation and dialogue. Review the sources identified in the textbook near the end of chapter 5 as guides to facilitation in preparation for the exercise. Divide up the class for a fishbowl exercise (half the class doing the exercise, the other half observing from an outer circle). Choose a "dialogue facilitator" to engage the part of the class doing the exercise in a discussion of a controversial or sensitive topic (e.g., the availability of abortion services; the right of women to cover their hair or not; the right of noncitizens to receive basic health and educational services; the easy accessibility of condoms or clean needles). After about 20 minutes of facilitated discussion, have the observers describe the positive aspects of the facilitator's work. Then switch groups, with the observers going to the center for the exercise and the other half of the class now becoming observers from the outer circle. Choose a facilitator and go a second round with a different controversial topic. Again, follow with a discussion of the positive aspects of the facilitator's work.

CLASS AND/OR COMMUNITY-BASED EXERCISE: TEACHING PRIORITY SETTING OR DECISION MAKING

Helping people to hear each other's perspectives and ideas is an important facilitation skill. Often the next step after hearing diverse opinions is to make decisions or set priorities. The skills and structures required to orchestrate fairness in decision making are valuable and important to level the playing field in group decision making. Learning the more formal processes for fair decision making can assist you in learning how to facilitate groups more equitably, even nonstructured groups that need to make decisions or set priorities.

Everyone has been a participant in a group meeting where decisions are made by majority vote and nearly half the group goes home disgruntled. Or where the "usual suspects" dominate the discussion prior to the vote—those who are the loudest, most eloquent, and most long-winded—influencing a perceived bias in the voting process. Decision making in structured settings has resulted in the most satisfaction by participants (Delbecq, Van de Ven, and Gustafson 1975). Delbecq and his colleagues developed a particular structured process during the years of the War on Poverty in order to provide the opportunity for people from all income and social levels in a community to come together and make decisions. The goal was to develop an equitable process that would help the majority of participants feel the process was fair, even in cases where their position on the issue was not selected in the voting process. The process was the Nominal Group Technique (NGT). With enough trained facilitators and scribes (one facilitator and one scribe needed for each group of five to nine people), and a sufficient space and tables for each participating small group, as many as one hundred people can engage in this process at one time.

This technique has been used by thousands of groups since then and has been modified in many ways while always retaining the fairness principles that guide the discussion, suggestion of ideas, and voting. You can find the guidelines for conducting NGT in the 1975 book by Delbecq, Van de Ven, and Gustafson, and you can also find a number of guides based on this process on the Internet. One such site is the Center for Disease Control Evaluation Briefs (Brief #7, November 2, 2006, at http://www.cdc.gov/HealthyYouth/evaluation/pdf/brief7.pdf).

A variation of NGT is Cardstorming, which has the advantage of moving the brainstorming group farther along in clarifying and clustering problems or issues. A disadvantage is that the group can be no larger than about forty people. Everyone must be able to see notes posted on a wall from where they are seated.

Using either NGT or the Cardstorming process, facilitate a brainstorming, priority-setting exercise. Practice both exercises first in the classroom and critique the usefulness of the two different methods. Then, engaging with a group of which you are a member, or a community group that has invited your facilitation, practice either one of the methods again to help the group brainstorm or prioritize issues they may wish to identify.

The following directions explain the process for carrying out a Cardstorming exercise.

THE CARDSTORMING PROCESS—FACILITATOR'S GUIDE

CREATED BY JAN SCHOPLER, PAUL CASTELLOE, AND DOROTHY GAMBLE

1. Ahead of time, engage with group/community leaders to identify the statement the group will use to stimulate the brainstorming activity. The exercise will work only if the leaders are convinced that the wisdom of the whole group or community is more valuable than the wisdom of an exclusive few. The leaders and the participants must also understand that "Cardstorming" is just the first step in a longer process that will require additional collaborative effort. The participating group can be as small as ten and as large as forty. The exercise takes about 1½ hours. It is good to have refreshments at the end to stimulate informal exchange among the participants.

2. Always choose a facility for the event that is neutral and public. All members of the community must feel comfortable in the space, and the facility must be accessible for all abilities. The space should be large enough so that the whole group can divide into smaller groups of about five people each and be able to hear each other in a discussion. A more diverse group will generate more and better ideas, as is true when using a Nominal Group Technique (NGT). Materials you will need on the day of the brainstorming event are at least four or five half sheets of letter paper (no smaller than 12×20 cm) for each participant and a marking pen for each participant. You will also need masking tape for posting ideas on a wall. If some participants are illiterate, or if you include some youth who are too shy to write, provide for a "recorder" for each group. This person will be responsible for writing down the individual ideas of all participants on the half sheets of paper. If the organization can afford the supplies, you can use 5×8 Post-it notes so that tape is not required.

3. Divide the large group into small groups of five people. Plan to have a trained facilitator working with each group. Also provide a recorder for each group if group members are likely to need assistance in writing down their ideas.

4. Begin with introductions to acquaint participants with each other and to focus on the topic. Next you will share the statement that you helped the group leaders to frame, which is the stimulus for the brainstorming exercise. For this exercise a statement that needs to be completed works better than a question that needs to be answered. (Allow 15 minutes for this process, or longer if you plan to allow everyone to introduce themselves.)

EXAMPLES OF STIMULUS STATEMENTS FOR CARDSTORMING:

- I'll know this community is safe for children when _____;
- I'll know our community is supportive of the elderly when _____;
- Economic opportunities are likely to increase in this community when _____.

5. The process facilitator should state and briefly comment on the following points (5 minutes) (it may also be useful to have the facilitator for each small group review them):
   - Everyone has important ideas to share and should participate.
   - Respect each other's ideas.
   - It's okay to disagree; in fact, different ideas should be encouraged.
   - Check to make sure everyone understands the statement.

6. Give people time to do their own thinking and write down their ideas independently. In this step all participants have time to individually

organize their thoughts before discussion begins in the small group. (10 minutes)

7. After each person has been allowed time to write his or her own ideas to complete the sentence, ask participants to share and discuss their individual ideas in this small group. Discussion often generates new ideas that no one had thought of earlier. Allow people to write down any new ideas stimulated by discussion. After discussion and addition of ideas, the small group can choose to consolidate some of the ideas if they seem very similar, or they can decide to put up all the ideas they generated. A single idea should be written on each half sheet of paper. Remind participants to write large enough so that everyone in the room can read from a short distance. It is also acceptable to tell each group they will be limited to six to ten ideas per group and so they have to choose the ones they feel most strongly about. Suggest the number of cards each group should produce, but don't be too rigid. (20 minutes)

8. Ask each small group to tape their ideas on the wall in the front of the room (or post all their Post-it notes on the front wall). Then select two volunteers from among all the participants to move the cards around, putting similar ideas in clusters as they are instructed by participants. Encourage all participants to point out similarities and suggest places to shift cards into "idea clusters." (This step has been done successfully with groups as large as forty, but the group has to be able to read the cards from where they are sitting, or they can stand close to the wall and move about looking for cards that best fit certain "idea clusters.") (25 minutes)

9. When all the ideas have been taped in clusters, the facilitator engages the group in discussing the connections among cards and asks the group to come up with labels for the idea clusters. The facilitator should write the labels suggested on cards and tape them above clusters. (10 minutes)

10. As the discussion proceeds, group members should check out the meanings of words and add ideas on new cards if important ideas have been left out. Refine "labels" for clusters. Discuss why specific ideas are important. Examine differences as well as similarities. As the discussion concludes, summarize and check with participants to ascertain whether the representation on the wall accurately reflects their thinking.

At the conclusion of the last three steps, you will have all the ideas generated by the participants in addition to having them sorted into clusters. (5 minutes)

TIPS FOR FACILITATORS

- Carefully think through the statement that is to be completed with the group leadership. Completing a **statement** and thereby affirming something seems to work better than responding to a **question**. The statement completion creates a "futures" picture of what the participants would like their community, region, or the world to look like.

- If you are using half sheets of paper rather than Post-it notes, prepare an adequate number of tape strips in advance. These can be lined up on tables near the wall. It saves time and confusion.
- Be sure to remind people to keep their ideas to three or four words and to **write large** so that later during the clustering step all participants can see all ideas.
- Be sure to allow 3 or 4 minutes for individual brainstorming after posing the statement; otherwise, some participants won't have time to collect their thoughts, and their wisdom will be lost if they don't participate.
- If you bypass the small-group discussion and just present the statement to the larger group, you will be less likely to get everyone's ideas, and a few people are likely to dominate the discussion.
- Ask participants to cluster the cards and rearrange them or tell the facilitator exactly where to place them—this is a group decision. The facilitator shouldn't be the one to organize the cluster ideas but instead should ask questions to clarify meaning and help the group come to a consensus.
- The next steps after Cardstorming should be worked out in advance with the organization/community leadership. Participants should know how the ideas that were generated will be used and how they will be involved in any activity to take the ideas to the next step (e.g., using the ideas to set priorities for community improvement; using the ideas to form action committees; using the ideas to organize new services or programs; etc.). Conclude with a question about implications and what the next steps should be. This gives people a chance to see the value in their thinking together.
- Keep additional cards handy to use in labeling clusters of ideas.

ADDITIONAL READING TO HELP YOU UNDERSTAND NGT AND CARDSTORMING:

Delbecq, A. L., A. H. Van de Ven, and D. H. Gustafson. 1975. *Group Techniques for Program Planning: A Guide to Nominal Group and Delphi Processes.* Glenview, IL: Scott, Foresman and Company.

Kaner, S., with L. Lind, C. Toldi, S. Fisk, and D. Berger. 1996. *Facilitator's Guide to Participatory Decision-Making.* Gabriola Island, BC: New Society Publishers.

Kramer, M. W., C. L. Kuo, and J. C. Dailey. 1997. "The Impact of Brainstorming Techniques on Subsequent Group Processes: Beyond Generating Ideas." *Small Group Research* 28(2): 218–242.

Schwarz, R. M. 2002. *The Skilled Facilitator: Practical Wisdom for Developing Effective Groups,* 2nd ed. San Francisco: Jossey-Bass.

Slocum, R., L. Wichart, D. Rocheleau, and B. Thomas-Slayter, eds. 1995. *Power, Process and Participation: Tools for Change.* London: Intermediate Technology Publications.

Timmel, S., and A. Hope. 1995. *Training for Transformation, Revised Edition.* Vols. 1–3. Gweru, Zimbabwe: Mambo Press.

VeneKlasen, L., and V. Miller. 2002. *A New Weave of People, Power and Politics: The Action Guide for Advocacy and Citizen Participation.* Oklahoma City, OK: World Neighbors.

6

ORGANIZING FUNCTIONAL COMMUNITIES

In this chapter we focus on the development and successful efforts of functional communities, those community groups that form because of a common identity or common interest or cause. In addition to understanding how these organizations are similar as well as different from other community groups, we emphasize the roles functional community groups play in the analysis of and advocacy for social justice and human rights. Functional community groups may be professional identity groups, such as organizations of social workers, which advocate for standards of practice and resources for clients, and they also include groups such as Amnesty International, which advocate for the freeing of prisoners of conscience anywhere in the world. We have therefore identified critical skills for community practice with functional communities to be the analysis of human rights and social justice issues; working, writing, and speaking as an advocate; and building leadership and networking skills. The exercises that follow focus on these skills.

SMALL-GROUP EXERCISE: DEFINING FUNCTIONAL COMMUNITIES

List community groups with whom you have had some contact that are organized because the members are connected by a *common identity* (e.g., women's organization, LGBT group, indigenous people's group, social work group, etc.). Then, list community groups with whom you have had some contact that are organized by people who share concern for a *common cause or interest* (e.g., anti–nuclear weapons group, support of military families group, antitrafficking group, human rights group, etc.).

- In your small groups compare differences and similarities between these two kinds of functional communities (i.e., identity groups and interest groups). Explore the vertical linkages of these groups to determine how they may or may not be connected from local to regional, national, or international networks. Discuss the particular advantages or disadvantages of deeper vertical networks. How will communication media differ across these vertical levels? What impact do you think Internet communication and the operation of "virtual communities" have on functional community groups?

- Now, consider the differences between these functional communities you have listed and the neighborhood groups that were the focus of the previous chapter; in particular, compare and analyze the meaning of membership, direct and indirect connections, and purposes and goals of the different communities. What are the most significant differences between neighborhood communities and functional communities?

SMALL-GROUP ACTIVITY: ANALYZING HUMAN RIGHTS AND SOCIAL JUSTICE ISSUES

In chapter 6 of the *CPS* textbook, we have presented two possible frameworks to assist in the analysis of human rights and social justice issues. One of these frameworks is adapted from Finn and Jacobson's (2008) use of *meaning, context, power, history*, and *possibility* to determine the basis of injustice and possibility for change (*CPS*, p. 184). The other draws on the work of two sets of authors, Cohen, de la Vega, and Watson (2001) and VeneKlasen and Miller (2002), to set out a plan for analysis of injustice and to explore options for change (*CPS*, p. 195).

- In your small group, look at the two frameworks in chapter 6 of the textbook. Compare the approaches. Determine which parts of each framework seem to be essential in your own efforts to analyze social justice issues.

You will be in a better position to compare these two frameworks if you have already spent time becoming familiar with the Universal Declaration of Human Rights and some of the international conventions and covenants identified by the IFSW/IASSW "Ethics in Social Work, Statement of Principles," http://www .ifsw.org/en/p38000324.html.

SMALL-GROUP DISCUSSION: FUNCTIONAL COMMUNITY ADVOCACY

The following case example describes an ongoing advocacy effort focused on building citizen and state legislative support for a bill to prevent bullying in the public schools. Discussion questions follow the case example.

EQUALITY NORTH CAROLINA—BUILDING SUPPORT FOR THE SCHOOL VIOLENCE PREVENTION ACT

SETH MAID AND STEPHEN WISEMAN

Equality North Carolina (ENC) was founded in 1979 and is a statewide group dedicated to securing equal rights and justice for lesbian, gay, bisexual, and transgender (LGBT) people. It seeks to achieve these goals by effectively lobbying the North Carolina General Assembly, executive branch, and local governments on issues including inclusive antibullying policies, employment discrimination, hate violence, privacy rights, sexuality education, adoption, domestic partnership, HIV/AIDS, and more. They also work to engage North Carolinians with educational programming and outreach efforts. Equality NC is the only statewide group focused on LGBT policy.

ENC has helped to introduce a bill called the School Violence Prevention Act (SVPA) in the North Carolina General Assembly. This legislation would standardize antibullying policy in all public schools (grades K–12) in North Carolina, and specifically prohibit bullying based on a list of enumerated categories, including sexual orientation and gender identity. The inclusion of these categories is important because studies have shown that students are ultimately better protected from harassment when they attend schools that have bullying policies with enumerated categories. As a southern state, North Carolina can have a somewhat conservative political landscape. Therefore, the inclusion of these particular categories has been controversial.

In order to achieve this change effort, the agency adopted several different strategies. ENC, a small organization of only four staff members, realized they could not accomplish this alone. Because the bill included a diverse grouping of protected categories (including race, disability, and physical appearance, among others), ENC staff knew they might be able to engender widespread support. We began to reach out to other progressive advocacy and community organizations making common cause, with the intent of building a large coalition in support of the bill. In deciding on possible partners, we reached out to organizations with a long history of supporting either LGBT rights or the rights of children. Using a mix of already established personal contacts, we set up meetings with various organizations to discuss common goals and strategize. Some of the organizations that became early partners with ENC included the Arc of North Carolina, a disability rights organization; the American Civil Liberties Union; and Planned Parenthood of Central North Carolina. Once these organizations agreed to be part of the coalition, they used their own contacts to connect with more institutions and agencies to bring them on board.

Although the inclusion of sexual orientation and gender identity in the bill may have limited the number of supportive agencies, ultimately over forty groups pledged their support for the School Violence Prevention Act. The bill became more controversial, because of the inclusion of sexual orientation and gender identity. However, participating organizations believed that it was important to protect all children, especially those most at risk of being bullied. In much the same manner, ENC first reached out to potentially supportive state legislators through a mix of personal meetings, phone conversations, and lobbying visits. We then partnered with these legislators, along with our coalition members, to help convince undecided legislators that the controversial aspects of the bill were not as important as the safety of all children.

CONTINUED

ENC also realized that to pass this legislation, efforts must be made to educate the public on the importance of the bill. We held several town hall meetings across the state, both in order to fully explain the need for comprehensive and specific bullying legislation and to recruit volunteers for the next phase of the change effort. ENC initiated a massive postcard campaign petition in which citizens from all across North Carolina signed postcards pledging their support for the School Violence Prevention Act. The postcards would then be hand-delivered to state legislators, providing them with tangible evidence of support from their own constituents for the enumerated categories in the bill. An added benefit of this campaign was that it enabled ENC to expand its e-mail contact list significantly, as those who filled out the postcards provided e-mail addresses. The postcards were to be delivered to legislators on a staggered schedule, in an effort to consistently remind legislators of support for the bill.

ENC also used its annual Lobby Day, in which LGBT individuals and straight allies meet with their legislators to discuss issues important to them and promote passage of the bill. Talking points were given to participants so that they were better able to discuss the School Violence Prevention Act, particularly the critical need to include enumerated categories of children likely to be at particular risk for harassment and bullying. ENC also utilized several Web-based media strategies for the first time. The organization promoted the legislation on Facebook, a popular social networking site, reaching hundreds of new individuals across the state. Another benefit of using this site was that ENC could quickly e-mail supporters of the legislation to keep them updated on the bill's progress and seek ongoing support. We also encouraged supporters to upload videos of themselves sharing their own experiences with being bullied to the video-sharing site YouTube. These communication methods both enabled citizens from all across the state to participate in advocacy efforts and helped to educate the broader public about the bill and its importance.

The North Carolina General Assembly finally took up the legislation in the spring of 2009. ENC and allies retained optimism and hope for passage of the act even in the face of considerable backlash from certain legislators and special interest groups. Harsh questions were raised about why the bill should include any categories of children and why "special protection" should be given to children with regard to their sexual orientation and gender identification. Negative comments made by members of the General Assembly and opponents of the bill received increased coverage in the media.

ENC and its allies continued direct advocacy work with members of the legislature, and continued campaigns to get citizens to send support letters for the bill to their representatives in the North Carolina House and Senate. These support efforts continued throughout the spring into late June. The North Carolina Senate, after much debate, passed the School Violence Prevention Act on May 6, 2009, by a final vote of 26–22. The bill then went to the House, where opponents continued to try to amend the legislation and distort its purpose. ENC, coalition members, and allies in the legislature fought hard to keep the bill intact and fully inclusive. Finally, on June 23, 2009, after two consecutive days of 90-minute debates on the merits of the bill, the House approved the intact School Violence Prevention Act by just one vote, 58–57.

The bill was signed into law by Governor Beverly Purdue on June 30, 2009. The School Violence Prevention Act has become the first pro-LGBT legislation ever passed in North Carolina, making it a significant and historic moment for the state. For the first time, some LGBT North Carolinians will enjoy equal protection under the law.

CONTINUED

Soon, the next stage of work to protect children from bullying begins: to work with schools and school systems to develop and implement sound administrative policies for enforcement of the law and protection of children at risk. ENC looks forward to both helping with this process and continuing to advance LGBT equality in North Carolina.

DISCUSSION QUESTIONS

- Describe the leadership role played by the staff of Equality North Carolina in this case example.
- Describe the critical collaboration and networking activities that were part of this advocacy campaign. How were these effective in building support for the legislation?
- Consider the prevailing culture for acceptance and protection of LGBT school-age children in your community. How would you frame the message to promote legislation to prevent violence and bullying in schools? Where would you find allies in your community to help you spread the message of such a campaign?
- Discuss the ways that Equality staff used multiple media to communicate and involve new allies for the antibullying bill, including several Web-based media strategies—creating both a "face-to-face" functional community/ad hoc coalition *and* a "virtual" functional community/coalition. What differences in advocacy and coalition building will these Web-based strategies make in the future?

INDIVIDUAL/CLASS ACTIVITY: PRACTICING ADVOCACY

Advocacy is often a part of working with functional communities as they develop agendas for improving conditions, responding to unmet needs, and creating a more just society. In this advocacy skill–building exercise, students will have an opportunity to develop a message for change. Using the ten points for guidance elaborated by VeneKlasen and Miller, write a formal news release or a letter to the editor about a current issue related to poverty, racism, or a discriminatory issue in your community (or in your country). Make sure you shed "light" instead of "heat" on the topic. That is, use logic and careful reasoning to make your points rather than confrontational statements that will make readers angry and thereby diminish the effect of your viewpoint. Carefully structured opinion pieces can persuade people to adapt and even change negative opinions—and that should be the goal. Bring the finished product to class to share with your classmates. If the letter is published, bring the published version as well. In your discussions analyze your own advocacy statement in light of the ten points advocated by VeneKlasen and Miller (2002, p. 232):

1. Know your audience.
2. Know your political environment and moment (e.g., controversies, big issues, fears, and what is considered left, right, and center).
3. Keep your message simple and brief.
4. Use real-life stories and quotes.
5. Use precise, powerful language and active verbs.
6. Use clear facts and numbers creatively (but accurately).
7. Adapt the message to the medium.
8. Allow your audience to reach their own conclusion.
9. Encourage audiences to take action.
10. Present a possible solution.

DISCUSSION QUESTIONS

- Who will see your letter? (How large is the media circulation, and who is likely to read it?)
- How are people likely to respond to the letter/news release you have written?
- How do you feel about taking a public stand on this issue?

REFERENCES

Cohen, David, Rosa de la Vega, and Gabrielle Watson. 2001. *Advocacy for Social Justice: A Global Action and Reflection Guide*. Bloomfield, CT: Kumarian Press.

Finn, Janet L., and Maxine Jacobson. 2008. *Just Practice: A Social Justice Approach to Social Work*, 2nd ed. Peosta, IA: Eddie Bowers Publishing.

VeneKlasen, Lisa, and Valerie Miller. 2002. *A New Weave of Powers, People, and Politics: The Action Guide for Advocacy and Citizen Participation*. Oklahoma City: World Neighbors.

7

SOCIAL, ECONOMIC, AND SUSTAINABLE DEVELOPMENT

In this chapter we focus on community practice that will result in improved social, economic, and environmental well-being, especially for the most vulnerable populations. The kind of development that connects all of these arenas, or at least seeks to know how development in one will affect the others, is called "sustainable development." Sustainable development recognizes the integration of social, economic, and environmental resources and has the goal of restoring and improving the resources in all three spheres simultaneously. Historically, social work has been more recognized for work in social development. More recently, social development efforts have taken on broader concerns for the economic well-being of populations, recognizing that social and economic conditions are tightly bound. Since at least 1992, and building on the discussions at the Earth Summit in Rio de Janeiro, environmental resources and degradation have been clearly linked to the social and economic conditions of human populations, especially very-low-income populations. Currently there is greatly increased scientific research, scholarship, and broader media coverage of issues of sustainability for our planet. This awareness has particularly focused on the role of human relationships in affecting social, economic, and environmental resources. Attending to new research, scholarship, and information, community practitioners now understand these complex issues, ideas, and interrelationships more deeply. In this chapter we encourage you to join practitioners in this vital work, taking on a broader view of development work. It is nearly indisputable now that work toward improved well-being in one of these arenas (social, economic, environmental) will affect the other two. The problems communities face now are complex and often have roots in all three areas. Ethically and professionally we cannot evade the responsibility to work across boundaries and seek solutions that can maximize social, economic, and environmental well-being. Simply replacing a closed factory with another pollution-emitting industry may provide some work and thus improve the social and economic conditions of a community. But the new industry may continue to pollute the air and water, contributing to increases in asthma, lung diseases, and cancer for the people who live there. Because of the complexity of development work, there is increasing recognition that teams of professionals from a variety of disciplines will be much more effective in solving integrated social, economic, and environmental problems than will any one professional working alone.

The exercises that follow will assist community practice workers in engaging with the more complex sustainable development concepts and the requisite measures that can indicate improvement, especially for the most vulnerable populations. The exercises also continue a deepening of understanding relating to human rights and social justice.

INDIVIDUAL EXERCISE FOLLOWED BY GROUP DISCUSSION: UNDERSTANDING ELEMENTS OF WELL-BEING

In this chapter we review the definitions of social, economic, and environmental well-being that were presented in chapter 1 of *CPS*. The elements of social and economic well-being are obviously creations of human societies and will be as diverse as human ingenuity and human cultures make them. Consider the definitions below with a focus on your *personal* well-being.

1. *Social well-being:* the ability of all people to have access to the supports and opportunities provided by social institutions and relationships. In other words, everyone should have access to supportive families, neighborhoods, and communities. Everyone should have the opportunity to engage in education, recreation, cultural organizations, spiritual institutions, and political organizations. In addition, following the perspectives of Richard A. Couto and Catherine S. Guthrie, families, neighborhoods, and communities can reinvest in future generations only if they have access to publicly supported institutions that contribute to health, welfare, education, security, and political processes. See their 1999 book, *Making Democracy Work Better: Mediating Structures, Social Capital, and the Democratic Prospect* (Chapel Hill, University of North Carolina Press).

2. *Economic well-being:* the opportunity for all people to achieve a wide variety of livelihoods and to ensure that wages pay enough to meet a family's

needs for shelter, food, health care, and transportation. Livelihoods are ways of life as opposed to jobs. Livelihoods encompass all the striving people do for themselves, their families, and their communities. Economics relates to the production, distribution, and consumption of commodities and services, including opportunities for paid and unpaid work, wealth, assets, and income. Economic considerations determine values for such things as care giving by parents and extended family members for children and the elderly, the work performed by formal and informal teachers, local farmers' organic produce, a work of art, the volunteers who deliver meals to people who are not ambulatory or are frail elderly, or planting trees in a public park. Civilizations value all of these strivings, yet economic formulas often undervalue or entirely exclude the value of some of them.

3. *Environmental well-being*: a condition that allows all people to have clean water and air and to have access to natural resources, ecosystem services, and the beauty of nature. The resources include all the elements of the biosphere we use or affect in the creation of our social and economic worlds.

- Describe your own well-being by identifying indicators that help you determine the relative positive or negative aspects of your well-being in the social, economic, and environmental arenas.
- Now, choose a part of your community (e.g., village, town, section of the city) that you believe has either a much higher or a much lower level of well-being than your own. Describe the indicators that help you determine the level of well-being for that part of the community.
- Discuss these perspectives with members of your small group to determine the different indicators people use to define their own well-being and the well-being of other people in the community.

INDIVIDUAL EXERCISE AND SMALL-GROUP DISCUSSION: RELATIVE WELL-BEING FOR HUMAN POPULATIONS

Earth Quiz for Social Workers (Prepared by M. E. Cox, Dorothy N. Gamble, and Emily R. MacGuire)

Complete the following quiz to test your knowledge. The answers are at the end of the quiz.

1. 187 member countries have ratified the United Nations Convention on the Rights of the Child. Name two countries that have not yet ratified this convention. (CRIN 2007)

   a.   b.

2. How many children between the ages of 5 and 14 work as child laborers in the world? (ILO 2006)

   a. 2,800   c. 28 million

   b. 28,000   d. 280 million

3. What is the average infant mortality rate (deaths per 1,000 live births) of developing countries compared to industrialized nations? (UNICEF 2006)

   a. 15 vs. 9   c. 159 vs. 50

   b. 59 vs. 5   d. 50 vs. 129

4. Approximately how many people die each year in developing countries from curable diseases? (World Revolution 2007)

   a. 170   c. 170,000

   b. 1,700   d. 17 million

5. What portion of the earth's resources is controlled by the richest 20% of the world's people? (Global Issues 2007)

   a. 17%   c. 53%

   b. 36%   d. 86%

6. In 2001, the number of people in the world who lived on less than $2.00 a day was _____ billion. (World Bank Group 2007)

   a. 0.7   c. 2.7

   b. 1.7   d. 3

7. U.S. drivers consume roughly __ % of the world's gasoline to propel 5% of the world's population. (Population Connection 2007)

8. On average, how many acres per person are required to support the lifestyle of a person living in the United States? (Environmental Almanac 2007)

   a. 4   c. 14

   b. 10   d. 24

9. According to Redefining Progress's latest Footprint Analysis, humanity is exceeding its ecological limits, and therefore the earth's biocapacity, by _____ %. (Redefining Progress 2007)

   a. 10%   c. 39%

   b. 25%   d. 50%

10. How many people in the world have no access to clean, safe drinking water? (UNDP, Human Development Report 2006)

    a. 500,000   c. 50 million

    b. 1 billion   d. 200 million

Answer Key

1. Somalia and the United States are the only two countries yet to ratify the CRC.
2. d. 280 million (as a comparison, the total U.S. population is approximately 300 million)
3. b. 59 vs. 5
4. d. 17 million
5. d. 86%
6. c. 2.7 billion (half the world's population)
7. 43%
8. d. 24
9. c. 39% (in other words, the earth plus more than another one-third of an earth)
10. b. 1 billion

RESOURCES

All information retrieved October 2007 unless otherwise noted.

Central Intelligence Agency. 2003. *The World Fact Book.* https://www.cia.gov/library/publications/the-world-factbook/index.html.

The Child Rights Information Network (CRIN). http://www.crin.org.

Earth Day Network. 2007. *Ecological Footprint Quiz.* http://www.earthday.net/footprint/index.asp#.

Environmental Almanac. 2007. *Ecological Footprint Analysis: Stepping toward Sustainability.* http://environmentalalmanac.blogspot.com/2007/01/ecological-footprint-analysis-stepping.html.

Global Issues. 2007. *Causes of Poverty.* http://www.globalissues.org/TradeRelated/Facts.asp.

International Labour Organization. 2006. *International Labour Conference Provisional Record.* http://www.ilo.org/public/english/standards/relm/ilc/ilc95/pdf/pr-15.pdf.

Office of the United Nations High Commissioner for Human Rights. 2004. *Status of Ratifications of the Principal Human Rights Treaties.* http://www.unhchr.ch/pdf/report.pdf.

The Population Connection. 2007. *Fact Sheet: Population and the Environment.* http://www.populationconnection.org/.

Redefining Progress. 2007. *Sustainability Programs: Ecological Footprint Quiz Based on 2002 Calculations.* http://www.rprogress.org/ecological_footprint/about_ecological_footprint.htm.

United Nations Development Programme (UNDP). 2006. *Human Development Report 2006.* http://hdr.undp.org/.

UNICEF. 2006. State of the World's Children. http://www.unicef.org/sowc06/pdfs/sowc06_table1.pdf.

World Bank. 2007. *About Us: What Is the World Bank? Strategic Direction.* http://www.worldbank.org/.

World Bank Group. 2007. *PovertyNet: Understanding Poverty.* http://web.worldbank.org/WBSITE/EXTERNAL/TOPICS/EXTPOVERTY/0,,contentMDK:20153855~menuPK:373757~pagePK:148956~piPK:216618~theSitePK:336992,00.html.

World Resources Institute. 2007. http://www.wri.org/.

World Revolution. 2007. Retrieved October 18, 2007 from http://www.worldrevolution.org/projects/globalissuesoverview/overview2/BriefPeace.htm.

- Reflect on the Millennium Development Goals that are listed in chapter 1 of the *CPS* textbook (table 1.1) or at http://www.undp.org/mdg/basics .shtml. The Millennium Development Goals were created in response to the current major development challenges faced around the world. Compare the items in the Earth Quiz with the Millennium Development Goals.
- Now, choose a finding from the Earth Quiz that you would like to improve.
- If you could change conditions, making improvements on the item you chose from the Earth Quiz, how many of the Millennium Development Goals might you also improve?

INDIVIDUAL EXERCISE AND GROUP DISCUSSION: ECOLOGICAL FOOTPRINT EXERCISE

Go to the Redefining Progress Web site to complete the Ecological Footprint Quiz: http://www.myfootprint.org/en/. The purpose of the quiz is to examine how much land and water you need to support your current lifestyle and understand what this consumption pattern means to you and people across the globe. In small groups of three or four, discuss the following questions after completing the Ecological Footprint Quiz:

- What implications does this information have for you personally? For others in your neighborhood, town/city, country, world?
- How could you use this information in your professional development?
- How is this information related to social work values, especially human rights and social, economic, and environmental justice?
- How does this information apply to the social work Code of Ethics in your country? To the IFSW/IASSW Ethics in Social Work: Statement of Principles?
- Each group member should summarize the points of the discussion that are most salient for themselves and write a brief paper that describes how this information will affect their personal behavior and inform their professional social work development.

SMALL-GROUP DISCUSSION—RIPPLES FROM ECONOMIC ADVOCACY: THE SANTA FE LIVING WAGE CAMPAIGN

Read the case example at the end of chapter 7 in CPS, "History of the Living Wage Campaign in Santa Fe, NM, USA" by Carol Oppenheimer. In small groups respond to the following questions:

- How does the increase in the minimum wage, which appears to be focused solely on economic well-being, also relate to social and environmental well-being?
- In this economic advocacy example, what are the important lessons to be learned for helping groups plan for taking action?

INDIVIDUAL REFLECTION PAPER AND SMALL-GROUP DISCUSSION: DEFINING EVALUATION INDICATORS FOR IMPROVED SOCIAL, ECONOMIC, AND ENVIRONMENTAL WELL-BEING

Design the lean framework of a hypothetical community practice project, briefly identifying only the location, goals, and outcome measures for the project (for the full model, refer to figure 1.2, Continuous Sustainable Community Development, in the *CPS* textbook). Assuming you have skillfully engaged the fullest participation of the people who will benefit from this project in its planning, a next step might be to help them identify evaluation benchmarks. How would you now coach them to identify and incorporate evaluation indicators that are representative of complex sustainability measures (i.e., measures that include at least two aspects of the three well-being arenas—social, economic, and environmental) rather than simple single-dimension measures? How will you help them see the value of measures that integrate social, economic, and environmental outcomes?

In preparation for your coaching sessions with community representatives or the community as a whole, review Hart's examples of Sustainable Community Indicators at www.sustainablemeasures.com, as well as indicators used in the Human Development Index from the most recent *Human Development Report* at http://hdr.undp.org/en/.

In discussion, compare your "coaching" and planning strategies with those of other members of the class.

INDIVIDUAL EXERCISE: PRINCIPLES FOR IMPROVED WELL-BEING

Write a brief paper that sets down the personal and professional principles that might guide your community practice work toward improved social, economic, and environmental well-being. In doing so, review the principles of Richard Falk, Richard Estes, Manfred Max-Kneef, and Vandana Shiva, cited throughout the *CPS* textbook. You may also wish to consult Nancy L. Mary's *Social Work in a Sustainable World* (Lyceum Books, 2008), as well as draw on the wisdom of persons from your region who speak or write about social justice and human rights issues that have an effect on well-being.

SMALL-GROUP DISCUSSION: UNDERSTANDING SUSTAINABLE DEVELOPMENT

Review the information about Hart's "Community Capital Triangle," and Gamble's "Moving toward Sustainability" models in chapters 1 and 7 of the *CPS* text (reprinted here as figures W7.1 and W7.2). Reexamine the two diagrams to sharpen your understanding of the meaning of *sustainable development*. Then form small groups to discuss the diagrams and the questions that follow them.

FIGURE W7.1 Hart's Community Capital Triangle

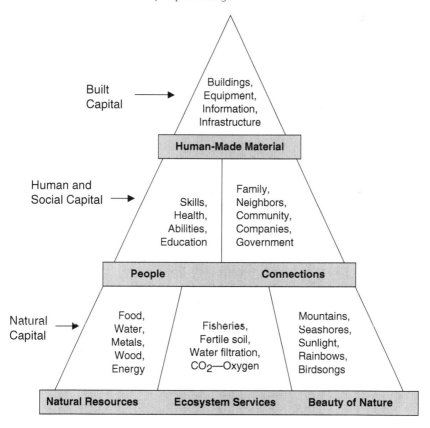

Community Capital

Source: Maureen Hart (1999), *Guide to Sustainable Community Indicators*, 2nd ed. (North Andover, MA: Hart Environmental Data), p. 16. Available from Sustainable Measures: www.sustainablemeasures.com. Used with permission.

FIGURE W7.2 Human Interaction toward Sustainability

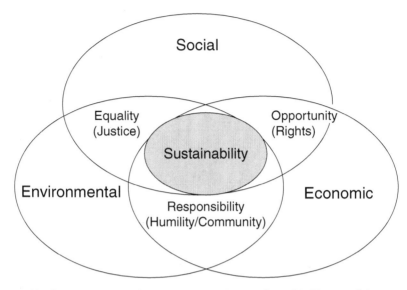

Moving toward sustainability: Human interaction with life-sustaining spheres of social, economic, and environmental resources

Source: Dorothy N. Gamble.

QUESTIONS FOR DISCUSSION

- What specific conceptual understandings from these two graphic models might you incorporate into your own work in community practice?
- In which of the three levels of community capital, or the three life-sustaining spheres, would you like your professional practice to have the most progressive results?
- In what ways can you measure how the progressive results you will have in one level or sphere will affect the other two?
- How can you direct your personal and professional behaviors, actions, and practice to reflect equality, opportunity, and responsibility as defined in Gamble's "Moving toward Sustainability" model?

8

INCLUSIVE PROGRAM DEVELOPMENT

This chapter emphasizes the importance of shifting from the traditional expert-based program development model to an inclusive model that stresses the engagement and active participation of local community members who, along with their families and neighbors, are intended to benefit from the planned program change. The inclusive model does not discount the experience and expertise that can be provided by community practitioners/planners, organizational members, or expert planners. Indeed, a balance of expertise is a hallmark of this model. Community members bring particular expertise about their community and environmental, physical, economic, and social issues and concerns, and some will likely have considerable experience with planning and development. Community practitioners and planners bring their own experience, along with technical, planning, interpersonal, and facilitative skills. The question is not "*Who* is the expert?" but rather who among us has the most useful expertise in "*What?*" Mutual, inclusive planning is the goal of this model. The chapter in *CPS* discusses the stages, tasks, and processes of inclusive planning. The content and exercises in this section of the workbook focus on giving you practice with visioning, planning roles, self-assessment, creativity in program design, creative presentation of community issues, comparison of the advantages and disadvantages of planning models in different contexts, and assessing specific sample components of a proposal to fund a community education project.

CASE STUDY FOR USE IN CLASS DISCUSSION: VISIONING TO EVALUATION

The following case example describes the highly participatory development of a program to serve HIV/AIDS survivors in a small town in western North

Carolina. The follow-up discussion questions focus on the roles taken on by the social worker in this case and how he used specific roles and skills to facilitate the involvement of the community of HIV/AIDS survivors and their allies who would benefit from the program planning effort.

THE HOSPICE PROGRAM AND PEOPLE LIVING WITH AIDS
FROM MARIE WEIL (2005), *THE HANDBOOK OF COMMUNITY PRACTICE*, USED BY PERMISSION OF SAGE PUBLICATIONS.

Kevin Branch had been a staff member of a local hospice (which was the only hospice in a three-county area) in western North Carolina since he received his BSW. After entering a part-time MSW program, he continued to work with Hospice as his field placement. When he had first started to work at Hospice, Kevin had been painfully aware of the number of people being referred who were dying with AIDS. In earlier years, it had not been uncommon for young gay men from rural western North Carolina to move to larger cities for work and partly to avoid the stigma prevalent in their home communities. Years later, following the epidemic-level progression of HIV/AIDS, a considerable number of these men had "come home to die"; and, for many of them, to find reconciliation with their families—and hopefully with some members of their communities. The Hospice program began to provide services for a number of these men who had chosen to die at home with their families and for some who were hospitalized.

Several years later, staff found that health clinics and other service providers in surrounding counties were continuing to refer everyone with HIV/AIDS to Hospice. However, these new clients were not dying of AIDS. Due to new medications and improvements in treatment, they were **living with AIDS**. It became clear to Kevin that Hospice services—focused on helping people have a good death—were not appropriate for these AIDS survivors. He began to talk with the men who had been referred regarding their real needs for support and services. He documented their responses, and proceeded to meet with other agency and community groups about the good news of much better survival rates and the service needs that the men had reported for themselves and their families. Slowly, a coalition began to develop that included members who were living with AIDS, family members, physicians and other health care providers, heads of citizens groups and civic organizations, and representatives from a number of human service agencies.

The group undertook efforts to identify additional people living with AIDS in the town and surrounding areas and did brief service assessments with them. Because people living with AIDS were conducting the interviews, potential respondents were not fearful about sharing their concerns. This assessment process and interviews with health providers revealed a much larger population of persons living with AIDS than had been referred to Hospice, and the informal coalition recognized that they had documented a major unmet need for support, services, and care.

After widening their circle of concerned citizens and professionals, the group requested a meeting with city and county councils to discuss this need and their assessment; they also approached small community foundations to seek support for develop-

CONTINUED

ment of appropriate services. Rather unexpectedly, several councils expressed more positive concern than had been anticipated, and while some groups were opposed to any public involvement in the issue, the positive responses began to reveal that the toll of AIDS deaths had already affected many families in the area.

Kevin and the coalition group were asked by three council groups to develop a specific plan documenting need and designing appropriate services. In this planning process they again sought information and counsel from the community of AIDS survivors and their families, from a larger number of health care providers, and from civic leaders. The plan was completed with a full report of the needs assessment, program and service design, and budget for four years of operation of an AIDS Support and Service Program that would work with persons living with AIDS to provide needed services, handle referrals, and provide support groups for victims and family members.

Over the three-year period that Kevin was in the MSW program, he and members of the coalition were able to obtain funding from three of the five local governmental councils and two small foundations. Kevin and another Hospice staff member became the director and program manager of the new nonprofit, WNCA, and began to implement the program with the help of a board, advisory board, and a number of community volunteers. In the third year of operation, the new organization was recognized by the regional United Way and gained more sustainable funding.

DISCUSSION QUESTIONS

1. In chapter 2 of the CPS text, table 2.1 identifies the following roles generally associated with inclusive program development: spokesperson, planner, evaluator, manager, director, proposal writer, trainer, bridge-builder, and visionary (see table 2.2 for role definitions). Which of these roles did Kevin Branch use in the course of developing the new program? How did he employ them?

2. Which roles were most effective for the program's successful evolution? Why?

3. Identify other roles you think would have been useful in this practice situation and explain how they could have improved the planning process and contributed to program success.

INDIVIDUAL ACTIVITY: COMMUNITY PRACTICE— LEADERSHIP DIMENSIONS REFLECTION

Complete the self-assessment in figure W8.1 individually, considering how a program manager/planner/director would use this activity to reflect on preferable leadership styles for inclusive program development. Bring the completed assessment to class and be prepared to discuss the results of your reflection.

FIGURE W8.1 Community Practice Self-Assessment Dimensions Reflection

Numerous assessment tools are available in print that can guide you in assessing particular technical skills. The following worksheet, adapted slightly for a community focus from the "Nonprofit Leadership Assessment" developed by Mathieu Despard, draws on other literature and has a different purpose. It provides you with the opportunity to assess complex issues such as self-awareness, communication and other interpersonal skills, values, and responses to conflict and visioning. Using this "softer skills" assessment can assist you in refining your skills in working with community members, coalitions, interagency groups, and staff groups.

Complete the assessment individually as a homework assignment to allow sufficient time for reflection. Bring it back to class with a copy for yourself and for your instructor. In groups of three, discuss the issues that interested or concerned you the most. While you do this, your instructor can list commonalities from the assessments (on newsprint/easel paper) so that the entire group can discuss and develop strategies to strengthen skills in these critical areas.

EMOTIONAL SELF-REGULATION AND AWARENESS

Ability to control or redirect disruptive impulses and moods. Ability to suspend judgment—to think before acting. Ability to recognize and understand your moods, emotions, and drives, as well as their effect on others.

		DO WELL	DO SOMEWHAT WELL	DO NOT DO WELL
1.	When I become upset in community or organizational work situations, I am able to delay actions until I am calm (i.e., I do not immediately react).			
2.	When someone upsets me in community or organizational work settings, I am able to refrain from hostile, insulting, or sarcastic comments.			
3.	When I am in a bad mood, I am able to prevent my mood from affecting interactions with community members or staff (i.e., others are not distracted by or concerned about my mood).			

INTERPERSONAL RELATIONSHIPS/COMMUNICATION

Ability to effectively engage others in community programs and projects through active listening, respect for divergent ideas and perceptions, and clear, purposeful, and transparent communication.

		DO WELL	DO SOMEWHAT WELL	DO NOT DO WELL
4.	I am able to communicate my concerns, interests, and intentions openly with others (i.e., I do not conceal information in an attempt to control communication) without becoming upset, agitated, sulky, or aggressive.			

		DO WELL	DO SOMEWHAT WELL	DO NOT DO WELL
5.	When members of community or organizational groups are sharing an idea or concern, I am able to focus completely on what they are saying, reflect what I heard, and ask for clarification if needed.			
6.	In facilitating group meetings, I work to see that all members have opportunities to participate. When communications of others are not clearly understood, I work to acknowledge their point and reframe the statement if needed.			

INCLUSION, PARTICIPATION, AND DECISION MAKING

	Ability to invite multiple stakeholders into and facilitate a process of shared and inclusive decision making.			
7.	In community and organizational settings, I am able to recognize when diverse stakeholder groups (members, other citizens, donors, board members, volunteers, staff) need to be part of a decision *and* am able to construct an appropriate opportunity/venue for this participation to occur.			
8.	I understand when I need to make a decision and I do it without needless consternation and delay. I am able to assist groups in using structured decision-making processes to assure fair and equitable participation.			
9.	When making an important decision, I gather information and consult with others to make sure I am making an informed and well-thought-out decision (yet absent unnecessary delay—see above).			
10.	In group settings, I do a good job of soliciting opinions, ideas, and concerns of others, even if this means withholding my own ideas or insights. I am able to facilitate group meetings so that participation is equitable and diverse positions are heard.			

RESPONSES TO CONFLICT

	DO WELL	DO SOMEWHAT WELL	DO NOT DO WELL
Ability to constructively engage in conflict using active listening, negotiation, and problem-solving skills. I am able to assist groups in understanding diverse positions and resolving conflict.			
11. I am okay with conflict—I see it as an inevitable part of the human condition. I recognize that as a community practitioner, I may be a target of conflict and I may have responsibility for helping groups to find ways through conflict—or "agree to disagree."			
12. In a conflict situation, I am able to help others identify and express underlying interests as opposed to stated positions.			
13. I am able to recognize when mediation or negotiation is appropriate and to participate in or facilitate negotiations between parties engaged in conflict.			

ETHICAL REASONING AND MORAL COURAGE

	DO WELL	DO SOMEWHAT WELL	DO NOT DO WELL
Ability to identify the legal and ethical dimensions of conflict and/or problems and to exhibit moral courage by taking a principled and ethical stand even at personal expense.			
14. I use a framework to help make ethical decisions (i.e., understanding choices, reviewing similar situations, consulting laws and regulations, identifying reasons and values for my preferred course of action, etc.).			
I am able to assist groups in conducting ethical analyses of problematic situations or choices.			
15. When there is clear wrongdoing in an organization or within a community project (e.g., sexual harassment, racial discrimination, theft), I am able to confront it, even if it means the possible loss of status, position, and/or friendship.			

VISION AND RESULTS

		DO WELL	DO SOMEWHAT WELL	DO NOT DO WELL
	Ability to conceptualize the long-term end result of a community program or project consistent with its stated mission. Ability to maintain a steady focus on intended outcomes consistent with this vision and to help others envision and focus on desired outcomes.			
16.	I can verbally articulate a vision for change consistent with the community or organization's mission that is compelling, inspiring, and easily understood by others.			
17.	I am able to maintain a steady and unwavering focus on the intended results (outcomes) of a program, project, or other set of activities and am able to help others gain and maintain this focus.			

Source: Developed by Mathieu Despard as the Nonprofit Leadership Assessment for the SSW University of North Carolina Chapel Hill; adapted slightly for a community focus by the authors. Mr. Despard relied on and adapted materials from the following sources: J. A. Ayres (2005), Leadership Self-Assessment; D. Goleman (November–December 1998), What Makes a Leader? *Harvard Business Review* 93–132; UNC School of Social Work (2007), Leadership Domains and Competencies (working draft); U.S. Office of Personnel Management, Executive Core Qualifications, retrieved on November 13, 2006, from www.opm.gov.

SMALL-GROUP DISCUSSION: SKILLS REFLECTION

1. In small groups of two to three students, discuss the differences group members identified in their self-assessments and ideas for how to strengthen skills in areas of concern.
2. Which skills identified in the assessment are ones you need to acquire in order to become an effective planner/manager/director?

SMALL-GROUP ACTIVITY: CREATIVE PROGRAM DEVELOPMENT

As we have described in various parts of the textbook, culturally appropriate art, theater, music, and humor are very effective in spreading the word about new programs and services. Sometimes even taboo subjects that require broad dissemination can be effectively opened for discussion using comedy, music, and theater. During her Peace Corps service in Niger, one of the authors, Emily MacGuire, observed the positive influence of theater and radio programming for spreading educational messages to a variety of communities. She created basic health education messages in the form of theater presentations with another volunteer. Together with a little comedy, they disseminated messages throughout rural villages and health centers about maternal health topics, including breastfeeding, malaria prevention, and the nutritional benefits of vitamin A. She further translated these skits into daily radio shows aimed at behavior change communication that addressed issues such as family planning, early marriage, hygiene, and childhood immunizations.

DESIGN YOUR GROUP PRESENTATION

Building from Emily's program innovations, design a group presentation with your small group. In teams of three to four, choose a local example of an underutilized service or sometimes sensitive program or service (e.g., condom use, antismoking campaigns, breast and prostate cancer screenings, reproductive health, mental health services, etc.). Design a 15-minute presentation in the form of a youth theater, puppet show, radio program, or other creative format. Plan and rehearse with your team outside of class. Bring back the skit/program to perform for the class.

For inspiration with this exercise, take a few minutes to look at the following interview and video with Mozambiquean singer Feliciano Dos Santos, who promotes village health through songs, humor, and information on the health advantages of installing EcoSan toilets: http://www.pbs.org/frontlineworld/stories/

mozambique704/interview/santos.html and http://www.pbs.org/frontlineworld/ stories/mozambique704/video/video_index.html.

CLASS DISCUSSION: COMPARING PROGRAM DEVELOPMENT APPROACHES

Inclusive Program Design: From Vision to Valuation (table 8.2 in the CPS textbook) is a melding of several program development models, drawn primarily from Linnell et al. (2006), Kettner et al. (2008), Netting et al. (2008), Pawlek and Vinter (2004), and Weil (2005). To understand and make use of this program development model, discuss the comparative advantages and disadvantages of the Basic Rational Program Design (table 8.1), the Interpretative Planning Process (table 8.3), and the Inclusive/Participatory approach as presented in the CPS text.

GROUP ACTIVITY

In small groups review the major attributes and advantages of each of the three program design approaches. For each approach—rational, interpretative, and inclusive—draft a brief description of a program and a list of factors reflecting its community context that is a good fit with the selected approach. For each program example develop a paragraph that explains why your group would use the approach selected for that program and community. Share your ideas, particularly the rationale for your group's choices, with the whole class.

INDIVIDUAL ACTIVITY: ASSESSING A PROGRAM DESIGN AND PROPOSAL COMPONENTS

Using the eighteen steps of table 8.2 in CPS, review and assess the following example of a program design and components of a proposal for funding. The proposal elements presented include a brief program description, needs assessment information, a logic model, outcome statements, a proposed program budget, and a program implementation timeline. Prepare your assessment as an individual written class assignment and later share your ideas in class discussion with two student recorders documenting points on easel paper. As a class combine and compare points mentioned by class members for each of the specific proposal documents. Then analyze the merits and potential problems of the proposed program itself and discuss the process and documents usually required to prepare a proposal for funding.

CASE EXAMPLE: PROMOTING MATERNAL AND INFANT HEALTH IN RURAL NIGER (PMIH)

EMILY MACGUIRE

Program Description: PMIH

The proposed three-part program will include antenatal education at the village level, midwifery training for selected villagers, and the elimination of clinic visit fees for pregnant women. Villages located more than 10 kilometers from the local health clinic will be randomly selected for participation in PMIH. First, the program team will hold community meetings to introduce the topic of antenatal care and gain buy-in for lessons and training from the villagers. In the selected villages of intervention, trained project team members will provide culturally appropriate education sessions for men and women concerning the importance of antenatal care. They will also encourage each village women's group to identify two women to attend a PMIH-run midwifery training program at the local clinic. A PMIH trainer based at the local health clinic will teach evidence-based best practices regarding village-level antenatal care to the selected group. Annual refresher trainings will provide the opportunity for all trainees to share their experiences and hone their skills. The PMIH trainer will also visit the trainees in their villages for follow-up meetings and consultations. At the clinic level, the program will introduce the elimination of visit fees for pregnant women who access antenatal services. The Nigerien government will be responsible for subsidizing the clinic fees. The central goal of the program is to reduce the barriers to accessing prenatal care for women in rural villages in Niger.

Needs Assessment for PMIH Rural Niger

Like much of the developing world, Niger is plagued by a weak public health infrastructure that is inadequate to meet the needs of the country's population. The lack of antenatal health care in rural areas of Niger highlights this dire situation. According to the 2008 *State of the World's Children* report from UNICEF, Niger has the highest total fertility rate in the world and antenatal coverage is estimated to be only 46 percent (United Nation Children's Fund 2008). The risk of death from pregnancy-related causes during a woman's lifetime is one in seven in Niger, compared to one in 4,800 in the United States and one in 17,400 in Sweden (World Health Organization, United Nations Children's Fund, United Nations Population Fund, and World Bank 2007; World Health Organization 2007b). These statistics demonstrate the need for a change in the Nigerien health care system.

Access to antenatal care is an issue that merits testing because it is a fundamental right included in reproductive health. By definition, reproductive health includes the right of access to appropriate health care services that will help women safely navigate pregnancy and childbirth (Cook, Dickens, and Fathalla 2003). Myriad barriers preclude Nigerien women from their right to access antenatal care. These barriers include location, poverty, cultural traditions, lack of education, and unavailability of services. A previous research study conducted in three regional districts of Niger reports that "15% or fewer of the population living more than one hour away from the health facilities vis-

CONTINUED

ited the clinics, compared with between 20–45% of those living nearer" (Diop, Yazbeck, and Bitran 1995, p. 230). Poverty also represents a major barrier to accessing health care services in Niger. The gross national income per capita in 2006 was $830, and the total expenditure on health per capita in 2005 was $25 (World Health Organization 2007b). Cultural traditions can play a role in inhibiting access to antenatal care, as does lack of education. In Niger, 45 percent of men and 31 percent of women have attended primary school (U.S. State Department 2008). Lack of medical personnel also contributes to the unavailability of services for pregnant women. Currently, there are only two nursing/midwife personnel per 10,000 people in the population (World Health Organization, United Nations Children's Fund, United Nations Population Fund, and World Bank 2007; World Health Organization 2007a).

PMIH Logic Model

Many foundations, international organizations, and governmental funders now require the inclusion of a logic model in a proposal seeking financial support. The logic model in figure W8.2 depicts the inputs, activities, outputs, and outcomes necessary for the successful impact of the PMIH program.

PMIH Program Outcomes

In an era of increasing accountability, all program funders are primarily concerned about a project they invest in achieving its desired outcomes—that is, making the differences in people's lives and situations that the proposal claims it will. As the logic model illustrates, the program is expected to produce the following outcomes:

> *Immediate Outcomes*: Villagers report increased knowledge regarding the importance of antenatal care; program-trained midwives demonstrate increased skills in antenatal care services; local health clinic staff, in conjunction with Ministry of Health officials, agree to eliminate fees for antenatal care visits for the district.
> *Intermediate Outcomes*: Villagers report increased usage of the local health clinic for antenatal care; program-trained midwives report increased referrals to local health clinics for identified pregnancy complications; local health clinic staff report no problems with the elimination of fees for antenatal care visits; records document increased usage of antenatal services by villagers from program-selected villages.
> *Long-Term Outcomes*: The ten villages selected for program intervention report reduction in barriers to accessing antenatal care in the region; the planned "Scale up" program includes all regions.

PMIH Program Budget

For potential funders, the budget along with outcomes are critical components of any program proposal. Outcomes state what the program seeks to accomplish, and the budget explains what funding will be necessary to provide required resources—personnel and nonpersonnel—to achieve the outcomes. Review the Program Budget in figure W8.3 to assess its appropriateness and discuss the rationale for the budget categories.

CONTINUED

FIGURE W8.2 Logic Model for Promoting Maternal and Infant Health in Rural Niger (PMIH)

INPUTS

- Financial and administrative resources
- Transportation
- Staff: Program, training, field
- Training materials
- Political will

PROCESSES

- Develop culturally appropriate outreach program with village input
- Conduct outreach program
- Select trainees
- Conduct midwife training
- Conduct meetings with MOH and district health clinic staff

OUTPUTS

- Community members exposed to outreach program that provides information about importance of antenatal care
- Midwives trained in antenatal care practices
- Government and local health clinic officials eliminate ANC visit fees

OUTCOMES

- Increased knowledge of antenatal care practices for community members
- Increased skills regarding ANC practices for program-trained midwives
- Increased service to community members by program-trained midwives

IMPACT

- Immediate: increased usage of local health clinic for antenatal care
- Intermediate: increased referrals to local clinic by program-trained midwives for pharmaceuticals and pregnancy complications
- Long-term: sustained usage of local health clinic and program-trained midwives for antenatal care services

FIGURE W8.3 Proposed Program Budget: Promoting Maternal and Infant Health in Rural Niger (PMIH)

	Year One	
ITEMS	EXPENSES	
Personnel		
Staffing and Benefits		
Program Director	Annual Salary	
Other Staff: _____	in kind _____	
_____	_____	
_____	_____	
Subtotal Salaries	_____ $0	
Combined Benefits	Amount $0	
Consultants	Fees	
Intern _____	$0	
_____	_____	
Contracted Services	Fees	
Theater troupe	$25	
Trainers	$200	
SUBTOTAL SALARIES, BENEFITS, & FEES		$225
Nonpersonnel		
Facilities		
Rent	$1100	
Construction	_____	
Utilities	_____	
Equipment		
Office furniture	_____	
Computers	_____	
Software & licenses	_____	
Internet access	_____	
Other office equipment	$50	
Supplies		
Office supplies	_____	
Postage	_____	
Training materials	$250	
Printing	$800	
Miscellaneous		
Transportation	$1700	
Local travel	$300	
Insurance	_____	
Staff recruitment	_____	
Staff training & development	_____	
SUBTOTAL NONPERSONNEL		$4200
BUDGET TOTAL		$4425

Budget justification: The personnel costs for the PMIH program are included in the Medecins du Monde operating budget. The program intern will not receive a salary. Contracted services include a theater troupe to launch the village-level education program and two trainers for the midwife training. Facility costs relate to the housing rental for the program intern ($1,000 for four months) and training facility rental ($100). Office space and most equipment will be in-kind donations from Medecins du Monde. A nominal amount ($50) is requested for gasoline to run a generator for the purposes of viewing instructional videos at the midwife training and village education programs. Other training materials, including laminated photo books for the trained midwives, are included in the supply request. One round-trip plane ticket for the program intern and local travel for the trainers, midwife trainees, and the intern are included in the transportation costs.

Program Timeline

Many program funders require submission of a timeline to illustrate the order of steps in program implementation and the estimated time each program activity will take. Review the timeline in figure W8.4 and discuss any questions in class.

FIGURE W8.4 Program Timeline for Promoting Maternal and Infant Health in Rural Niger (PMIH)

ACTIVITIES	APRIL	MAY	JUNE	JULY	AUG.	SEPT.
Develop training materials	▓					
Select 10 villages for intervention	▓					
Develop outreach program with village input		▓				
Select 2 midwife trainees from each village		▓				
Rent training site location		▓				
Acquire instructional videos for programs		▓				
Conduct planning meeting with theater troupe		▓				
Conduct meetings with Ministry of Health and district health clinic staff about fee elimination		▓				
Conduct outreach education program in 10 selected villages			▓			
Conduct midwife training			▓			
Eliminate antenatal visit fees at regional health clinic			▓	▓	▓	▓
Evaluation and follow-up for outreach program				▓	▓	▓

FIGURE W8.4 *(continued)*

ACTIVITIES	APRIL	MAY	JUNE	JULY	AUG.	SEPT.
Evaluation and follow-up for midwife training program				▓	▓	▓
Evaluation and follow-up with health officials about fee elimination				▓	▓	▓
Staff Needs						
Hire project intern	▓					
Designate midwife trainers	▓					
Hire theater troupe	▓					

Resources

Cook, Rebecca J., Bernard M. Dickens, and Mahoud F. Fathalla. (2003). *Reproductive Health and Human Rights: Integrating Medicine, Ethics, and Law.* New York: Oxford University Press.

Diop, François, Abdo Yazbeck, and Ricardo Bitran. (1995). The Impact of Alternative Cost Recovery Schemes on Access and Equity in Niger. *Health Policy and Planning* 10(3), 223–240.

United Nations Children's Fund. (2008). The State of the World's Children 2008. Report. http://www.unicef.org/sowc08/docs/sowc08.pdf.

United Nations Population Fund. (2007). Contraceptives Save Lives Fact Sheet.

U.S. State Department. (2008). Niger. Retrieved July 5, 2009, from http://www.state.gov/r/pa/ei/bgn/5474.htm.

World Health Organization. (2007b). Statistical Information System, Core Health Indicators 2007. Retrieved September 14, 2008, from http://www.who.int/whosis/database/core/core_select_process.cfm?country=ner&indicators=healthpersonnel#.

World Health Organization, United Nations Children's Fund, United Nations Population Fund, and World Bank. (2007). Maternal Mortality in 2005. http://www.who.int/whosis/mme_2005.pdf.

World Health Organization. (2007a). Country Health System Fact Sheet 2006, Niger. Retrieved July 5, 2009, from http://www.afro.who.int/home/countries/fact_sheets/niger.pdf.

PROPOSAL PREPARATION

The proposal components presented here are only some of the essential parts of a proposal for program funding. You can expect that a proposal will be needed for any program that will require external resources. You will also often be expected to provide a diagram illustrating the program components and how they fit together; letters of support from people who believe that your program is needed and that it will work; an executive summary; and a letter of application. A number of books, articles, and Web sites discuss program design and proposal development, and we encourage you to read additional materials and assess additional examples.

ADDITIONAL PROGRAM DEVELOPMENT RESOURCES

- The following templates are useful resources for developing logic models: http://www.uwex.edu/ces/pdande/evaluation/evallogicmodel.html and http://www.wkkf.org/Pubs/Tools/Evaluation/Pub3669.pdf.

SMALL-GROUP ACTIVITIES

1. After completing your individual review/assessment and class discussion of the PMIH program example and its proposal components, divide into small groups of three to four students. As a small group, discuss the cultural context of the program model and how the elements of this model could or could not be translated across cultural groups and to villages or small towns in other regions of the world.
2. Select a program with which at least one of your group members has worked. Write outcome statements for that program using the PMIH outcomes as an example.
3. Think about ways to explain your program's impact on client groups, community, and community resources and construct your own logic model for the program your group is considering.

REFERENCES

Kettner, Peter M., Robert M. Maroney, and L. L. Martin. 2008. *Designing and Managing Programs*, 3rd ed. Thousand Oaks, CA: Sage Publications.

Linnell, Deborah, Zora Radosevich, and Jonathan Spack. 2002. *Executive Directors Guide: The Guide for Successful Nonprofit Management*. Boston: Third Sector New England.

Netting, F. Ellen, Mary Katherine O'Connor, and David P. Fauri. 2008. *Comparative Approaches to Program Planning*. Hoboken, NJ: John Wiley & Sons.

Pawlek, Edward J., and Robert D. Vinter. 2004. *Designing and Planning Programs for Nonprofit and Government Organizations*. San Francisco, CA: John Wiley & Sons.

Weil, Marie. 2005. "Social Planning with Communities." In *The Handbook of Community Practice*, ed. M. Weil, pp. 215–43. Thousand Oaks, CA: Sage Publications.

9

COMMUNITIES AND SOCIAL PLANNING

In this chapter we provide two case studies for you to analyze and critique. First you can compare and contrast a recent participatory budgeting project—in China—with the Porto Alegre, Brazil, case study presented in chapter 9 of the *CPS* text. Participatory budgeting gives the local community some control over some portion of the local budget. In thinking about the effects of context on program implementation, it is useful to examine distinctions and differences in approach in relation to national and regional differences.

The second case study involves you in analysis of a twenty-eight-year process of iterative planning that has evolved through organizing campaigns, and program and community development projects, all carried out to promote progressive social change. This case study involves you in examining both organizational and community development processes as the involved communities have sought to respond proactively to changing environmental, economic, and social conditions. Chapter 9 in the *CPS* text reports the "Lessons Learned" by the Center for Community Action and community groups in Robeson County from their long-term planning work. This further exploration allows you to witness the substantial social change produced through the planning and implementation of multiple, sequential community programs and projects.

CASE STUDY: THE IMPORTANCE OF PARTICIPATORY BUDGETING IN CHINA
EXCERPTED FROM A REPORT BY DR. CHEN JIAGANG OF THE CHINA CENTER FOR COMPARATIVE POLITICS AND ECONOMICS, BEIJING

The modern Chinese economic market system has been developing since 1978, and the growth of the economy has generally been steady—though sensitive to downturns in the global economy. The quality of people's lives has increased greatly, and China's

CONTINUED

growing economy has been gradually integrated into the world economy. At the same time, interesting political reforms have made progress as people began to elect their leaders directly at village and town levels—particularly in towns, cities, and villages where participatory budgeting has been adopted.

Citizens are involved in the political process through several kinds of participatory mechanisms. The main challenge that we are facing now in China's political reform is how to make democracy work. Based on the experiences in Brazil, we expect that adopting participatory budgeting at the local level will be helpful to promote participatory democracy in China.

Basic Information about Xinhe Town

Located in Zhejiang Province, Xinhe town was selected as the first target for participatory budgeting. It is in the northeast sector of Wenling city and has 89 villages and 6 city communities with a total population of 119,000. It was selected partly because of its industrial progress and stable agricultural production and partly because of advance preparation.

A specific intervention, "democratic consultation," involving local residents with outside consultants knowledgeable about democratic decision-making processes, was used to prepare and encourage citizen participation. Over several years, this education process was conducted to promote public dialogue and discussion between governments and citizens on public affairs, and to initiate a channel for citizens to participate in public administration at the grassroots level. Citizens' opinions and suggestions have had an impact on the decisions made by party committees and local governments. The process has also increased transparency in decision making, and helped to prevent decisions that would go against the interests of the majority of citizens. While there are still problems in these efforts, the introduction of participatory budgeting provides useful direction and guidelines to make the work of the township level People's Congress and citizen volunteers more democratic and inclusive.

DISCUSSION QUESTIONS

Why was "democratic consultation" from experts needed to help citizens in Xinhe engage in participatory budgeting?

What was done to prepare citizens in Porto Alegre?

What training would *you* need to engage in this process?

Emergence and Spread of Participatory Budgeting in Xinhe Town

Partly because of the town's multiyear training experience with democratic consultation in processes of dialogue, communication, and deliberation during policy making, the involved officials, elected representatives, and citizen volunteers were ready to get involved with participatory budgeting.

CONTINUED

In July 2005 Xinhe town's People's Congress first discussed the budget through democratic consultation. Deputies and other voluntary participants discussed reports on the executive budget and the draft of the new budget; they questioned it and forwarded many suggestions to modify it. They approved the budget based on the modified draft, and participatory budgeting was initiated.

In November 2005, a second budget meeting was held with 40 persons, including town congress deputies, members of the budget subcommittee, and voluntary villagers participating in the meeting. This marked the beginning use of everyday "checks and balances" on the budget. It also attracted scholars and officials from Beijing and Shanghai.

Process of Participatory Budgeting

The approach to participatory budget reform in Xinhe town abides by the following process:

- electing deputies of town People's Congress directly;
- drawing up the draft of the budget by town administration and submitting it to the congress;
- discussing the draft deeply among the deputies;
- interpreting the work of administration concretely; and
- expressing their ideas about it.

After this process, town administrators and the budget examination group modified the draft together according to these suggestions, formulated a new draft, and submitted it to the People's Congress once more for approval.

Now in Xinhe town, directly elected deputies participate in the process of administering the town budget directly. The whole budget process in the town is public to the deputies.

DISCUSSION QUESTIONS

1. Were these same processes followed in Porto Alegre?
2. How can participatory budgeting increase democratic decision making in communities?

Training to Increase Knowledge of the Budget and Rights

Before democratic consultation began, scholars from several universities with expertise in budgeting and the functions of congress were invited to Xinhe town to conduct a class on public finance training for deputies and villagers. The professors taught 80 participants that revenue was taxed from citizens and that government expenditures shall be public. Residents shall know how the money is spent and where they are in the process. They also taught participants about the principles and technical knowledge of drawing up a budget. The citizens also learned from them what the rights of citizens are, and how to express their ideas in the town's People's Congress.

CONTINUED

Following this training the democratic process consultation began and proved to be the key means to increase deputies' knowledge of budget processes and their comfort with participating in political processes. Training participants wanted to understand both the municipal budgeting process and People's Congress procedures. The new training enhances the capacity of deputies and citizens when they participate in the political decision-making process, express their preferences, criticize the administration, and provide suggestions for change. It is an important factor in the success of participatory budgeting in Xinhe town.

Achievements of Participatory Budgeting in China

From the participatory budgeting experience in Xinhe town, we can see results that have had positive effects on China's local reform and development of democratic processes:

- Promoting participation and transparency in political decision making
- Strengthening the power of deputies to check and monitor the budget
- Making the draft of the budget and procedures more detailed and transparent
- Fostering civic virtues necessary for participatory democracy.

Results: Providing More Public Services for Residential Areas

Since participatory budgeting began, the quality of life and provision of public services have improved throughout the town. There are more civically educated residents who are more active in community life. The administration and the congress spend more time discussing the public good and allocate more budget funds to public services such as road construction, clean water provision, school construction, garbage collection, and more services for residents.

These changes have especially benefited communities with the greatest needs and helped make service provision more equitable. The final point is that different countries can learn from each other during their experiments. The practices of different democracies can enrich the theory of democracy and promote the practices of democracy in the world.

CLASS DISCUSSION

Together identify twenty to twenty-five nations that use democratic governing processes. How would you describe or illustrate differences among democracies? Develop a class definition of *democracy*.

DISCUSSION GROUPS

Convene in groups of four and list the differences you think apply between the contexts for participatory budgeting in Brazil and in China. Then practice taking different positions on the following and/or your own ideas and questions:

1. How do differences in the political, social, and economic contexts between the two nations affect their implementation and outcomes of participatory budgeting?
2. What would it take to establish participatory budgeting in your own township or municipality? Share and compare your group's ideas with those of other class members.
3. Together discuss this question: What are some of the benefits of the participatory budgeting exercise that relate to community practice?

LONG-TERM MULTICULTURAL COMMUNITY PLANNING

The following case example from rural North Carolina explores the challenges and triumphs of inclusive multicultural community planning over twenty-eight years. This case should be used as a major focus for class discussion of community-based planning. A variety of interactive role plays can be developed. Specific programs developed can be examined through the CCA Web site. Group projects grounded in this case study can explore specific ideas and develop brief presentations about how to initiate planning processes and tasks for selected projects and programs—ranging from educational and political reform, to creation of the Family Support Initiative and subsequent collaborative projects, to establishing the River Way Outdoor Adventure and Education Center and Lumber River State Park—can provide challenging learning and planning simulation experiences. As a class discuss how you want to "mine" this long-term case example to learn in depth from its process of unfolding and transformative social change.

"WHAT WE CAN'T DO ALONE, WE CAN DO TOGETHER"—SOCIAL PLANNING AND SOCIAL CHANGE IN ROBESON COUNTY
MAC LEGERTON, EXECUTIVE DIRECTOR, THE CENTER FOR
COMMUNITY ACTION (CCA)

For nearly 30 years planning work facilitated by CCA has moved progressively forward in this highly multicultural (Lumbee Indian, African American, White, Latino populations) county of rural North Carolina. Long-term community-based planning is reiterative, with development of sequential programs, projects, and change strategies. Over time in Robeson County, both local contexts and concerns shifted, and people and collaborating

CONTINUED

agencies learned how to move from one project to the "next level" by leveraging resources and external supports, strengthening collaboration, developing coalitions, and building on the success of earlier programs and projects to create positive outcomes in succeeding work—expanding from organizing local programs for children to large environmental sustainability projects.

Robeson County is a place of contrasts. On the one hand, it has significant cultural and ecological assets, including a slow, winding river, 50 swamps that feed it, and an abundance of plants and animals. On the other hand, it is a place of significant poverty and is now ranked as the third poorest midsize county in the United States (U.S. Census Bureau 2009. State and County Quick Facts: Quick Facts about Robeson County, North Carolina, at http://www.google.com/search?client=firefox-a&rls=org.mozilla%3Aen-US%3Aofficial&channel=s&hl=en&q=U.S.+Census+Bureau%2C+2006+Robeson+County+North+Carolina&btnG=Google+Search).

CCA has played and continues to play a major facilitation and planning role in county-wide work for transformation in Robeson County. Three basic steps guide the social planning process at CCA. The first step is to see the situation and condition as it really is. The second is to see it as you desire it to be. The third is to determine what methods would lead to the desired aim. Both formal and informal research and reflection are key components of the entire social planning process.

Reflection is also key to every step in our deliberative process, which includes:

1. a deep and broad understanding of the root causes of social situations and conditions;
2. a clear vision of what the organization wants to do, where the gaps and barriers are in comparison to what other organizations are doing or able to do, and how to partner with them;
3. an analysis of the organization's needs and capacity to implement selected objectives and strategies; and
4. insight into the positive and challenging consequences of implementing and achieving our goals.

At the Center, social planning is not an end in itself; we use this process to build community and strengthen relationships across groups. The key to our planning work is that we utilize an empowerment process based on the participation and expression of the people's voices, opinions, feelings, and knowledge that comes out of their life experiences. Authentic planning and deliberation builds community and creates a shared identity and common purpose.

The affective and community-building aspect of planning and deliberation is rarely given significant attention in literature or technical trainings on strategic planning. When disagreements and discord occur and as issues and programs come and go, relationships and community building are the foundation of continued work and commitment.

". . . many of our original goals were achieved after almost 15 years. We found ourselves about 5 years ahead of our 20 year plan!"

Committed to the vision, values, and principles of love and social justice, CCA's original mission was to "organize and empower individuals, families, and communities to unite

CONTINUED

and improve the quality of life and equality of life in Robeson County, N.C." We began monthly meetings in various parts of the county in 1980, starting with a very diverse group of 25 people at our first meeting. At each monthly meeting, we asked questions related to causes of poverty and discrimination, as well as changes needed in institutional policies and practices to increase social, political, and economic opportunities.

The major social change needs and goals identified over the first three years of our work were:

- More professional and equitable racial representation in county and municipal government;
- More professional and progressive elected officials and administrators;
- Court and law enforcement reform—leading to a more balanced and fair system with more diverse leadership, including a Public Defender System;
- Education improvement and school reform, including school merger;
- Public assistance reform—better and broader delivery of services to the poor, sick, and needy;
- Employment reform—better wages, benefits, and working conditions;
- Economic development—more locally owned, small businesses;
- Agricultural reform—alternative crop production with less use of pesticides and herbicides;
- Environmental protection of our land, water, and wildlife;
- Cultural and multicultural curriculum in our schools; and
- Youth and adult leadership development.

We compared our findings from these discussions to U.S. Census and other published data on our county and state. We listed and sought out all the people and local organizations that could help change and improve our county. Over the years, more people came forward as leaders and contributors, many of whom we had not known before. We understood that it would take the hard work and cooperation of many groups, coalitions, collaborations, organizational leaders, and thousands of ordinary citizens to achieve our shared goals and that we would have to work on more than one issue at the same time. All of the problems and solutions that we identified and selected related to increasing equality and social justice in our county. We wanted to correct the historical imbalances in our local society by combining the strategies of planning, community organizing, grassroots empowerment, research, coalition building, and policy change.

We successfully developed short- and long-term plans for multiple projects, with a central goal to achieve equitable and fair treatment, representation, access to opportunity, and more equitable resource distribution in particular institutions and systems. Following almost 15 years of sustained work, many of our original goals were achieved; and, critically, all three major races were now equitably represented on our Board of Commissioners, School Board, and legislative delegation following successful redistricting projects. Our educational and legal systems had been reconstructed and improved. We merged the five separate school systems into one unit. We had halted three major toxic waste and low-level radioactive waste facilities from coming in and protected our river and wetlands by creating the Lumber River State Park. New leaders, including elected officials of all three major races, county, administrators, agency directors,

CONTINUED

and grassroots leaders from across the county, had more inclusive and creative visions and commitments. These diverse new leaders became partners with CCA in its major community development and systems change programs.

Strategy Change

As more of our social justice goals were achieved, we realized our assumptions and strategies needed to fundamentally change. We added new programs in family support, education advancement, health promotion, and sustainable development. Institutional leaders began asking CCA for help in bringing grassroots people, other agencies, and more diverse partners to the tables of decision making. With these requests, we expanded our facilitative and planning role into new sectors of social and economic development and justice.

Through our planning process we learned that our effectiveness and success were rooted in two complementary qualities:

1. our capacity to build and broaden our base and influence the grassroots community while expanding our base among professional service providers, community leaders, researchers, and policy makers; and
2. our capacity to adapt, broaden, and deepen our work in social planning based on what we learned from our experiences, constituents, and changed social conditions that had either a positive or negative impact on our families, communities, and social systems.

CCA planned and organized partnerships, bringing grassroots and professionals together to address major community needs and challenges. From youth development to environmental protection CCA brought diverse groups together and overcame insurmountable obstacles. From "we can't change this system" to "what we can't do alone, we can do together," a major cultural shift occurred and raised both our anticipation and achievement of crucial social change.

"Maximizing grassroots participation with multi-agency engagement . . ."

In 1994, Robeson County was selected as one of 16 counties to participate in a new Family Support and Family Preservation Program through the North Carolina Human Resources Division of Family Development. Because of our central role in multisector partnerships that were grounded in grassroots culture, I was contacted by the State Director of the Family Preservation Services Program to host an orientation meeting to begin local planning activities in our county.

The planning process, led by a community planning team from the UNC Chapel Hill School of Social Work, was a comprehensive process for the development of meaningful and responsive family preservation and family support strategies. The emphasis was on interagency collaboration, creation of a continuum of family support and preservation strategies, and involvement of culturally diverse families. Of the initial $25,000 grant, $5,000 was designated for incentives to support family participation in the planning process.

CONTINUED

CCA brought diverse grassroots leaders together with diverse agency leaders who shared grassroots perspectives. The organizations and agencies involved in the Family Support Program still include: the Health Department, CCA, Public Schools, the Department of Social Services, Mental Health Department, Juvenile Justice, and NC Legal Aid. The Board includes program participants, community leaders, and agency representatives.

Maximizing grassroots participation in the community needs assessment and planning process, CCA provided mini-grants that averaged $100 to 42 grassroots groups. Following training, they were responsible for facilitating the assessment, holding community meetings, and submitting their community assessments and findings. A total of 750 people attended the 42 community meetings and provided input on community problems, challenges, and available resources; they recommended solutions to meet community needs and solve problems. An additional 500 people filled out the community assessments and turned them in at various locations across the county.

The highly participatory planning process of the new Robeson County Family Support Program was the largest and most diverse community assessment and strategic planning program in the county's history. During the planning process, Robeson County Department of Public Health offered to administer the new program if CCA would manage its implementation and expansion.

Now in its 13th year, the Robeson County Family Support Program serves 350 families and continues its focus on parental engagement, becoming the largest child maltreatment prevention, family literacy, school readiness, and fatherhood program of its type in North Carolina. CCA selected grassroots outreach workers to recruit and support parents and professional teachers to deliver its 11-week curriculum. This creative combination of deep community outreach by grassroots workers and empowering curricula delivery by professional teachers has led to a high rate of retention, graduation, and parent and child satisfaction, learning, and bonding.

The successful collaborative work of the Family Support Program helped us to secure new resources and supports to develop or expand additional educational and youth programs, including the Learning Together Program, the Rural Education Advancement Program, and the River Way Outdoor Adventure and Education Center. *All of these projects are based on the model of public/nonprofit partnership developed through the Family Support Program.*

The Learning Together Program was awarded a major research grant from the W. K. Kellogg Foundation and is now an evidence-based project that has been tested and evaluated in 11 diverse sites throughout Robeson County. It now serves over 350 families and is the largest child maltreatment prevention and family literacy program of its type in North Carolina.

DISCUSSION QUESTIONS

1. Describe the types of communication skills needed by grassroots leaders and program managers to achieve the high levels of collaboration required to implement the Family Support and Learning Together programs.

2. How can collaboration and coalitions support the planning and implementation of complex programs in multicultural communities?
3. How would you encourage members of diverse groups to work together despite a history of racism and exclusion?
4. What supports are needed to help grassroots programs participate effectively in program intervention/outcome research?

New Learning, New Approaches

After years of work in successful education reform, we planned and implemented a new, multistrategy project entitled the Rural Education Advancement Program in 1997 in partnership with our local schools and with state and national educational programs, including the Partnership for Children and the Rural School and Community Trust. We focused on education advancement and policy change to introduce place-based and culturally based education practices and community-school partnerships. Through the Rural School and Community Trust, we joined the Native Sites Working Group and visited exemplary cultural- and place-based development programs across the nation.

Through this project, we connected with the Alaska Native Knowledge Network (ANKN) grounded in "Learning through Culture" (as contrasted with learning "about" culture). Visits to ANKN reinforced the realization that local groups can and do learn deeply from other engaged communities and that this process of mutual learning needs to be a central component of planning. We found that the most fruitful way to support mutual learning was to take people to visit other engaged communities and to learn from them through dialogue—listening to their stories, their struggles, and wisdom. On returning home we adapted and used successful, diverse models and practices; we "took the best and left the rest."

New Challenges and a New Planning Approach: "Research, Plan, Organize, and Strategize"

In the 1990s, when more inclusive and equitable representation in governance was achieved in Robeson County and attention was focused on economic and educational development, the economic foundation of the county was ripped away. The manufacturing and tobacco industries that had been the backbone of the county's economic sector for the past 50 years collapsed. With new federal trade policies that encouraged overseas investments, the county's economy was totally deconstructed. Forty percent of our for-profit sector was gone. It was as if, just when a new and common "table" for governance and decision making was created, the economic legs of that table were cut out from under its makers.

After watching over 8,000 jobs leave over the 10-year period from 1993 to 2003 and experiencing the social destruction that it caused to families and children and the pressures that it placed on the service delivery system, many people began discussing what could be done in a proactive way to counter this trend.

We knew that we had to research the impact of job loss, address economic development policy at all levels, and develop creative and proactive solutions. So, we went to work, utilizing what became a standard planning model for CCA: "research, plan, organize, and strategize" in a complementary, non-sequential order. We also had to decide which of the eight levels of transformation (individual, family, community, institutional, systemic, cultural, environmental, and moral/spiritual) we wanted to impact and which of the five major strategies (social relief, social support, social development, social reconstruction, and social witness) we wanted to use in order to impact them.

When we have not had the resources to develop needed programs and interventions, we identified partners who did. Our organizational and program planning was comprehensive, based on what our families and communities needed, rather than what our organization could do. CCA's plans focused on a major research project and report on the social and economic impact of our massive job loss, and a trip to Washington, D.C., to share the report and testify before Congress.

Utilizing an economic analysis and the identification of six major sectors in our economy that needed significant reconstruction, we recently developed a comprehensive plan for rural sustainable development in the county. The six sectors are: (1) education; (2) health; (3) agriculture and forestry; (4) manufacturing; (5) entrepreneurship and small business development; and (6) recreation and tourism. These represent two growth sectors (1 and 2), two challenged sectors (3 and 4), and two emerging sectors (5 and 6). People working in each sector are being organized. Sector leadership teams are planning and facilitating the development and implementation of strategies to reconstruct, expand, and sustain businesses and living wage employment in each sector. This work continues.

"We have achieved major successes . . ."

We have achieved major successes in Robeson County on all eight levels of transformation identified in this study. With effective and successful organizational and program planning and implementation, we have accessed the private and public resources necessary to support our extensive work and sustain it over the last 28 years.

SMALL-GROUP ACTIVITY

In small groups discuss, prepare notes on easel paper, and then report the organizational characteristics you think operated within CCA to make it possible for them to continue planning work, "roll with the punches," and find new and creative action strategies to deal with new problems. How can this long-term change approach be adapted to focus on planning, organizing, and development issues in inner-city neighborhoods?

SMALL-GROUP ACTIVITY

In groups of three or four, compare the planning skills and styles used in the Jacksonville case study from the CPS textbook and the CCA case study above. The Jacksonville Community Council used the rational planning approach, while CCA employed an inclusive approach. Identify differences in components, discuss differences in style, and list ways to determine when to use each approach.

CLASS ACTIVITY: STRENGTHS, WEAKNESSES, OPPORTUNITIES, THREATS—ANALYSIS

Many organizations and community groups use a particular approach to problem analysis, often called "strategic planning," when their organization faces one or more crisis situations, such as less funding, major political or context changes, population changes, or environmental changes, or when a judgment is made that the organization is not fulfilling its mission and goals. The following exercise, a SWOT Analysis, can be an important tool to use in thinking through organizational and community issues.

SWOT ACTIVITY ANALYSIS FOR A COMMUNITY SETTING

1. Place four large sheets of paper on the wall, labeled at the top "Strengths," "Weaknesses," "Opportunities," and "Threats."
2. Explain to the group that strengths and weaknesses refer to factors internal to their organization or agency and thus ideally within their control; opportunities and threats refer to forces in the external environment, such as a budget cut or a new, community-friendly mayor or city council that may influence the organizing issue at hand.
3. Give all participants several blank Post-it notes in each of four colors, using a different color for each of the four categories. Have participants think of important SWOT factors and write them on individual notes—for example, strengths on yellow, weaknesses on blue, and so forth.
4. Have team members place these Post-its on the appropriate sheets of chart paper.
5. As a group, look for common themes in each area and cluster items together by moving the Post-its around as needed. Add any new factors that come up and identify urgent or high-priority issues.
6. Stepping back, look at all four areas to identify strategic or critical issues that emerge from the discussion. A critical issue is typically a challenge, dynamic tension, or conflict around which change needs to occur. For

example, your environmental justice organization has just received a grant for neighborhood organizing (strength), a new incinerator is being proposed in a high-asthma neighborhood (threat), and a key planning commission official has been exposed for accepting bribes from the industry backing the incinerator (opportunity).

7. Look for a fit between different forces and your core issue. Prioritize strategic issues by importance and timing, decide what area to focus on, and brainstorm possible scenarios.

A thorough SWOT Analysis, when written up with strategies for action, is often the major component of a strategic plan.

10

BUILDING EFFECTIVE COALITIONS

oalitions are groups of organizations that have come together for a purpose, forming a network to build strength in numbers and pooling resources for short- or long-term associations. In chapter 10 we focus on coalitions that are organized to improve social, economic, or environmental conditions, especially for vulnerable populations. Working with coalitions requires considerable skill, resilience, and flexibility on the part of the community practice worker because of the complexities of managing groups that are autonomous, yet align themselves in associations to accomplish certain goals. We have identified ten guiding steps for working with coalitions in chapter 10 of *CPS*. In the following exercises we emphasize learning strategies for building inclusive coalitions, a model for a coalition advocacy event, and a personal audit for skill assessment.

FIELD INTERVIEW AND EXERCISE: BUILDING AN INCLUSIVE COALITION

As in all of the models we have discussed previously, building coalitions should be accomplished by drawing from the widest possible number of organizations to ensure a diverse and inclusive collaborative effort. This is not an easy task, and many coalitions are formed from among the people who are known as the dominant leaders in a community. Some coalitions are so committed to building diverse representation from the community that they refuse to fully organize until they are certain the coalition will represent people of color, women, elders, youth, and people who would benefit from the coalition's actions. The "Inclusivity Checklist" from Meredith Minkler, ed., *Community Organizing and Community Building for Health* (New Brunswick, NJ: Rutgers University Press,

2004), is a helpful guide to consider even before efforts to build a coalition have been undertaken.

In teams of two or three, arrange an interview with the leadership of a local coalition (e.g., organizer, chair, co-leaders, etc.). Ask if you can explore with them a discussion of coalition inclusivity, letting them know the interview will not be written up anywhere but that information from the discussion will be used as a classroom learning exercise. In your small interview groups discuss and outline the way you plan to begin, explain the purpose and format, and close the interview—including deciding who will ask which questions. Using the "Inclusivity Checklist" below as a guide in your interview, explore the strategies the coalition uses to be diverse and inclusive, and the barriers they find to accomplishing the goal of achieving diverse representation from the community. (If you cannot find a coalition to interview, use a class session to discuss possible strategies to meet the checklist goals.)

COALITION INCLUSIVITY CHECKLIST

- The leadership of our coalition is multiracial and multicultural.
- We make special efforts to cultivate new leaders, particularly women and people of color.
- Our mission, operations, and products reflect contributions of diverse cultural and social groups.
- We are committed to fighting social oppression within the coalition and in our work with the community.
- Members of diverse cultural and social groups are full participants in all aspects of our coalition's work.
- Meetings are not dominated by speakers from any one group.
- All segments of our community are represented in decision making.
- Coalition members are sensitive to and aware regarding different religious and cultural holidays, customs, and recreational and food preferences.
- We communicate clearly, and people of different cultures feel comfortable sharing their opinions and participating in meetings.
- We prohibit the use of stereotypes and prejudicial comments.
- Ethnic, racial, and sexual slurs or jokes are not welcome.

Checklist reprinted from Beth Rosenthal (1995), *From the Ground Up: A Workbook on Coalition Building and Community Development*, edited by T. Wolff and G. Kaye (Amherst, MA: AHEC/ Community Partners), 54–55, 69, by permission of the author and editors.

If you are successful in arranging interviews, share your results in a discussion with your classmates.

CLASS PROJECT: BUILDING A COALITION FOR AN ADVOCACY EVENT

The following exercise requires a significant commitment of time and effort. It could take from four months to a year, depending on the readiness of the community coalition to bring an issue to the front burner. The exercise will help you develop planning, managing, direct practice, and community organizing skills, all identified in chapter 10 of the *CPS* textbook as necessary skills for building effective coalitions.

A People's Hearing is a technique for helping groups advocate for an issue that is so deeply buried it will have a difficult time getting to the surface—or "on the table"—for consideration by governmental bodies and other decision makers. Sometimes it is an issue that policy makers really don't want to struggle with, and they are perfectly happy to keep it below the horizon. Or it may seem so complex and embedded no one wants to open it up. A People's Hearing is one way to shine light on an issue without being confrontational. It brings the issue out into the public arena for discussion. The technique was developed in 1971 by the National Welfare Rights Organization and has been used successfully by a number of different organizations since then.

Assuming there is an issue that the whole class, or part of the class, would like to advocate for, the first task is to determine whether an advocacy coalition already exists or whether an ad hoc coalition can be easily organized for the event. Before beginning, reread the ten "guideline steps" in chapter 10 that describe the process of building and nurturing a coalition. The process for carrying out a People's Hearing follows.

A PEOPLE'S HEARING: A CITIZEN-LED MODEL FOR STIMULATING COMMUNITY DISCUSSION ON COMPLEX ISSUES
ADAPTED FROM THE NATIONAL WELFARE RIGHTS ORGANIZATION

Often as we struggle in communities for better understanding of issues for which governments (municipal, state, national, and even international) intend to craft policy, the issues themselves seem too complex, too controversial, and too far removed from the experience of everyday citizens for reasonable involvement. This complexity often keeps citizens out of the discussion and out of the debate around policy options.

A People's Hearing differs from a public hearing in that it is sponsored by local citizens rather than an official government body. It is held in a public place to reinforce the idea that the public should have a say in the issues being discussed. Every effort is made to invite key decision makers and influential people in the community to be present as a **Listening Panel.** People who are knowledgeable about the issues

CONTINUED

and might be directly affected by the issues are asked to comprise the **Witness/ Perspectives Panel.** They describe in a brief way how the issue at hand affects the general public. Following the presentations by the Witness/Perspectives Panel, the meeting is opened for general discussion. The Listening Panel is not required to speak, but they may comment and raise questions just as any other person who is sitting in the audience might. The steps below describe the process and explain its rationale.

1. **Who should sponsor the People's Hearing?** Any group of citizens may sponsor a People's Hearing. A collaboration of organizations is a stronger approach. Several organizations working together, somewhat like-minded in their belief that discussion of the issues is necessary and urgent, gets more people involved. It is also a way to incorporate organizations that might represent different perspectives and different parts of the community. (For example, a group interested in youth homelessness might want to involve homeless youth themselves, parent groups, health providers, school representatives, youth organizations, police, and arts and recreational representatives.)

2. **What should it be called?** The general name for this process is "A People's Hearing." Because so many good words in our society have been branded with bad connotations, it is important to look for a phrase that describes the meeting that is both specific enough to explain the intent and also sounds inviting/interesting. This is sometimes a struggle since the mobilization of bias about certain words makes it acceptable to call our missiles "peacekeepers" and peace organizations "unpatriotic." The important thing is to give the event a name that will draw people to the event. A coalition wanting to open the discussion about the need for legal domestic partnerships for members of the LGBT population, for example, might call their meeting "Commitments with Legal Rights" or "The Rights of All Families."

3. **Where should it be held?** Generally, the idea behind this format is to hold such a meeting in a public and easily accessible setting. This ensures that the public is clearly welcome and that people own public spaces. Generally, there should be no charge to participate. Holding such a meeting in a church, theater, or private meeting room suggests that the discussion is exclusive. Such a meeting could be held in a municipal, state, or community center, or a public school building.

4. **Invitations to the Listening Panel:** The Listening Panel should include municipal, state, and national elected officials, religious and spiritual leaders, owners and editors of media, and anyone else the organizing groups determine to be significant movers and shakers in opinion mobilization and actual policy determination. These people are asked to come to listen, not to speak. They are asked to listen to the ideas presented and the follow-up discussion of the audience. If they wish to participate as part of the audience they are most welcome. The Listening Panel members should be approached both in writing and personally. This helps to assure them that there is no intent to force them to make a statement in public. The reason the format asks the decision and opinion makers not to speak is that they have easy access to having their voices heard; however, too often the people are simply listeners. This format turns the tables and asks the decision and opinion makers to listen to the people.

CONTINUED

5. **Preparation of witnesses/perspectives and handouts:** Together, the coalition representatives that plan a People's Hearing should decide which are the most salient points to illuminate a discussion of the issues. There should be no more than six or seven major points of focus. Once the points are identified, individuals should be selected to prepare a presentation for each one of the points. The group of presenters should represent some diversity in the community. A mixture of Ph.D.s and self-taught presenters is usually more convincing, as well as being sure that young and old, different genders, cultures, and so on are represented. You may select some members of the populations who are "living with the issue or problem" and others who also have particular expertise, concern, or involvement in the issue. The presentations should be no longer than 5 minutes. Presenters can use handouts or graphics, paper copies of three or four PowerPoint slides, or even a short video to make their points. (A picture is always worth 1,000 words, and if you both hear and see something you have about a 50 percent retention possibility.) A rehearsal should be held to see if the points are well made and how effectively the whole issue is covered so that adjustments can be made and timing checked. Any material that could help the audience members and Listening Panel grasp the ideas should be prepared in advance as a handout.

6. **Moderator:** The moderator has a very important role. She or he will open the meeting, introduce the topic, serve as timekeeper for the Witness/Perspectives Panel, open the meeting for discussion following the presentations, explain to all attending how the meeting will be followed up, and close the meeting.

7. **Publicity:** The meeting should be publicized widely so that everyone understands it is open and that they are welcome. Prepare press statements early. Radio, newspapers, and Internet lists should be used, making sure to go more widely than the norm of usual channels so that the meeting will draw people who may not usually come to public discussions. If the presenters represent a wide swath of the community, that helps to draw in groups that represent the diversity of the community. Each collaborating group should make it a point to personally contact two other groups they are familiar with to invite their members to the "hearing."

8. **The event:** Think about the time of the event. If it is late, it may exclude some of the elderly who avoid night driving. If it is early, it will exclude the working people. If child care can be provided, it will be more likely that young families can attend. It must be in a location that is accessible for people with disabilities and those who depend on buses or bicycles for transportation. If parking is difficult, some form of carpooling may be organized. Serving refreshments after such a meeting encourages more informal discussion. All the collaborating groups could bring cookies and tea, or you could get local restaurants to donate some cookies. Involving different groups in tasks spreads the word through informal publicity. Schoolkids could produce artwork for the walls highlighting their vision of the community if the problem to be discussed did not exist. Consider these and additional ways to make the setting and event not only accessible but also welcoming and interesting with useful information materials available for everyone attending. It is important to keep the hearing process on the planned time schedule. No one goes away happy if

CONTINUED

FIGURE W10.1 Structure for a People's Hearing Event Held in a Neutral but Public Place

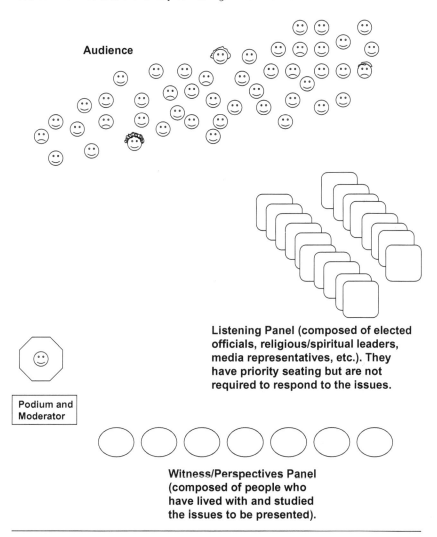

Audience

Listening Panel (composed of elected officials, religious/spiritual leaders, media representatives, etc.). They have priority seating but are not required to respond to the issues.

Podium and Moderator

Witness/Perspectives Panel (composed of people who have lived with and studied the issues to be presented).

they think the meeting has gone on too long. Announce, give out flyers, and have sign-up sheets for any follow-up activities that are planned.

9. **The follow-up:** Plan a follow-up letter to each member of the Listening Panel with the following message:

- Thank them for attending.
- Reiterate the purpose of the meeting.
- Ask if this format was a favorable way to enlarge understanding about important public issues for a wide range of people.

CONTINUED

- Ask if a smaller group of people could meet with them personally to discuss specific proposals relevant to the issues.

   Have a follow-up meeting of the People's Hearing planning group to evaluate the event and clarify or confirm directions for moving forward. It is important to remember that the purpose of this format is to engage the public in the issues and try to move the decision makers in the direction of responsible, progressive, sustainable policies. As we know, "if the people will lead, the leaders will follow." All the hopes of people for progressive change should not be lodged in changing the views of those in power; however, such a People's Hearing can start the process to educate, campaign, network, and propose policy options.

10. **Moving forward:** The People's Hearing format is effective for moving some community issues from the back burner to the front burner of public and governmental consideration. Other meeting formats can be effective for setting priorities on how to move forward on different fronts. Nominal Group Technique and a faster modification called Cardstorming (see chapter 5 of this workbook) are formats to establish priorities.

Figure W10.1 provides a graphic design suggesting the room/auditorium arrangement for a People's Hearing.

We hope that during your preparation for community work you will be able to work on organizing and holding a People's Hearing. While it takes considerable time and effort, it represents a good opportunity for service learning and may prove to be of lasting benefit to a community if it opens the doors of communication and builds support for issues that have been ignored by officials.

REFLECTION PAPER: KNOWLEDGE AND SKILLS AUDIT FOR COMMUNITY PRACTICE WITH COALITIONS

What do I need to do to prepare for working with multiple organizations toward shared change goals? How can I assist in building a coalition? How can I assist members of a new coalition in developing consensus about strategies and actions?

Use some of the following questions from the *CPS* textbook to guide your response:

- What are my understandings of and perspectives on the values and limitations of coalitions?
- What characteristics seem to identify coalitions with success in this community?

- What characteristics seem to deprive coalitions of power and legitimacy in this community?
- Which of the roles identified as important for working with coalitions (mediator, negotiator, spokesperson, organizer, bridge-builder, and leader) and skills (management, planning, direct practice, and community organizing) have I had experience with? In which roles would I have strengths? In which skills do I feel competent?
- What strategies and plans can I make to strengthen my skills for working with coalitions?

11

POLITICAL AND SOCIAL ACTION

Political and social action are joined in this model because most community work intended to improve economic, political, environmental, and social conditions eventually involves changing oppressive and discriminatory policies, and sometimes changing policy makers through campaigns and elections. Making changes through nonpartisan approaches, thereby holding any political party to a higher standard with regard to social justice and human rights, can be the best solution for achieving more lasting social improvements.

We begin our exercises with a focus on the Universal Declaration of Human Rights, understanding that it is an aspirational document and not a perfect one. It is, however, too little understood and appreciated by community practice workers who need to make use of it. Next we propose an exercise relating to the CEDAW, the Convention on the Elimination of All Forms of Discrimination Against Women, to emphasize our proposition that the expansion of rights for women and girls will benefit all societies and continue to influence community practice throughout this century. The next several exercises focus on policy changes, first exploring these efforts in two case examples, then allowing small groups to choose their own issue to explore policy change and campaigns to accomplish such change.

CLASS PROJECT: UNDERSTANDING, CRITIQUING, AND CELEBRATING THE UNIVERSAL DECLARATION OF HUMAN RIGHTS

The Universal Declaration of Human Rights (UDHR) has thirty articles. Review the history of its creation and the rights themselves at: http://www.un.org/

Overview/rights.html. Divide the class into small groups and assign each group a portion of the thirty articles until all articles are assigned.

SMALL-GROUP ACTIVITY AND CLASS ACTIVITY

- First, discuss the focus of the articles of the Declaration that have been assigned to your group. Which of the three categories of rights are represented in the articles your group is exploring? How many are "negative rights," or rights that ensure political and individual freedoms; "positive rights," or rights that ensure standards of services, opportunities, and resources; or rights that guarantee the collective and collaborative efforts among nations? Discuss the meanings of these articles for your location (i.e., community, country) in terms of their universal or relative acceptance. Explain how people actually access the rights described.
- Second, create a message board or poster with words, symbols, and culturally appropriate pictures that illustrate and describe the rights. Make one poster for each article of the Declaration your group has been asked to examine.
- Third, together as a class share and critique the thirty posters your class members have created. As the discussion progresses, have two students write on easel paper (1) potential contradictions identified between some articles; and (2) the possibility of cultural (e.g., Western) biases you think may exist.
- Fourth, display the posters, all thirty of them, on December 10, Human Rights Day, in a prominent location; have available "Birthday Card Handouts" containing the UDHR. (The UDHR was 60 years old in 2008.) If your class does not meet in December, find an appropriate holiday to display the posters, and be sure that they are exhibited again on the following December 10.

INDIVIDUAL REFLECTION PAPER: APPLYING ARTICLES FROM THE UDHR TO SOCIAL, ECONOMIC, AND ENVIRONMENTAL CHANGE

Choose a local condition / human rights concern that you believe is important to change in order to expand the ability of people to exercise that right and thereby improve social, economic, and/or environmental well-being in your area. In a brief two- or three-page paper:

- Describe the existing problematic condition.
- Choose the UDHR article or articles that are most relevant to the condition/problem, and analyze how the condition relates to those specific Declaration articles.
- Explore the condition or problem globally, either through the UDHR Web site listed above or through the WiserEarth Web site at http://www.wiserearth .org/, to find out what others are doing to help people in their communities attain and exercise the specific human rights you are exploring.

CLASS EXERCISE: UNDERSTANDING AND CELEBRATING THE RIGHTS OF WOMEN AND GIRLS

March 8 is International Women's Day. The celebration will commemorate its 100th anniversary in 2011. You can view recent global celebrations on the IWD Web site. With your class members visit the Web site for the Convention on the Elimination of All Forms of Discrimination Against Women (CEDAW) at http:// un.org/womenwatch/daw/cedaw/, and study the provisions of the convention.

In small groups of four or five prepare a 5-minute presentation that might be broadcast on a local radio station on March 8. Be creative with songs and radio drama to get the attention of listeners. Each group will present their message in class. Discussion on the methods and messages used will assist you in learning more about media presentations. Have a subgroup contact local radio or TV stations to see if you can persuade one of the local media outlets to broadcast your messages. Also consider placing videos of the messages on your school's Web site or seeing if local community-based organizations will sponsor them on their Web sites.

- If your country has ratified CEDAW, the focus of your broadcast will be on how women and girls can make use of the provisions in the convention to secure their own rights.
- If your country has not ratified CEDAW, your broadcast will focus on what women and girls could gain if the convention were ratified in your country.

SMALL-GROUP DISCUSSION: COMPARING APPROACHES TO POLITICAL ADVOCACY

Review the case example at the end of chapter 7 in *CPS*, "The Santa Fe Living Wage Campaign," and the case example at the end of chapter 11, "Durham CAN." In small groups:

- Discuss and illustrate how political advocacy (i.e., advocacy for policy change) was carried out in both cases.
- Compare the similarities and differences in strategies used to increase awareness in the community about the need for policy change.
- Explore the actions and strategies that were most important in accomplishing policy change in both examples.
- Discuss the strategies necessary to monitor and stabilize policy change once it has been enacted.
- Share the most salient points of your group's discussion with the entire class.

INDIVIDUAL STUDY AND SMALL-GROUP DISCUSSION FOLLOWED BY CLASS STRATEGY DEVELOPMENT: HOMELESS YOUTH—ANALYZING BARRIERS AND DEVELOPING STRATEGIES FOR POLICY CHANGE

INDIVIDUAL ANALYSIS—FIRST WEEK

- Locate the "Social Justice and Human Rights Analysis" framework in CPS, chapter 11 (p. 376). With a focus on homelessness among youth, analyze the economic, social, and environmental factors that operate as barriers at local, regional, national, and international levels to finding solutions for this social problem.
- For practice, choose a second problem that is important to you and do the same analysis, looking for economic, social, and environmental barriers to solutions at local, regional, national, and international levels.

ANALYZING BARRIERS AND PROPOSING POLICY CHANGE: SMALL-GROUP EXERCISE—SECOND WEEK

- Compare the economic, social, and environmental factors that serve as barriers to finding solutions to the problem of homelessness among youth at the local, regional, national, and international levels. Use newsprint or blackboard to list the factors identified by each member of the small group.
- Discuss with your group the most likely policy changes at local, regional, national, and international levels that could not only decrease the numbers of homeless youth in your area but also assist these young people to find a safe environment for their further development.
- As a full class, discuss and record how the policy changes class members propose may or may not connect to social justice and human rights concerns.

A class member can type up the group's recommendations and provide copies to class members as an example of one aspect of multilevel policy analysis and a document that provides information for policy advocacy talking points.

With regard to homeless youth, some resources for exploring this issue in the United States can be found at: http://www.endhomelessness.org/section/policy/focusareas/youth and http://esciencenews.com/articles/2009/01/29/perceptions.and.experiences.homeless.youth.vary.race.ucsf.study.shows.

VETERANS AND THEIR FAMILIES: POLICY ANALYSIS AND POLICY CHANGE

SMALL-GROUP EXERCISE—THIRD WEEK

Another issue that may be important in a number of countries is the marginalization and vulnerability of veteran soldiers and their families (see, for example, http://www.pbs.org/moyers/journal/05302008/profile3.html).

- Using the social justice and human rights analysis framework, members of the small groups work together to complete the analysis of problems faced by veteran soldiers and their families by listing the economic, social, and environmental factors that seem to be barriers to solving the problems these families face, whether they are lodged in local, regional, national, or international conditions and policies.
- Next, as a group, determine what kinds of policy changes at any level could lead to improvements in quality of life for veteran soldiers and their families. Make your suggested policy changes more focused by using Lisa VeneKlasen and Valerie Miller's SMART objectives criteria: objectives for desired change should be specific, measurable, achievable, realistic, and timebound (see their book, *A New Weave of Powers, People, and Politics: The Action Guide for Advocacy and Citizen Participation* [Oklahoma City, OK: World Neighbors, 2002]). Use these criteria to outline recommended policies and their intended outcomes.
- Finally, as a group, outline or diagram proposed actions to organize and carry out a nonpartisan campaign to influence the policy changes your group recommends. You might again use guidance from VeneKlasen and Miller (2002) to elaborate your campaign, taking note that changes must occur in the government arena, private sector, civil society, political spaces, and individuals to accomplish transformative change.

12

MOVEMENTS FOR PROGRESSIVE CHANGE

In this chapter we highlight examples of social movements we believe are congruent with the values of social work—for example: fair trade and fair wages, civil rights, peace, and public control of water. We introduce several more examples, such as the efforts to stem the destructive oppression of poverty and to promote positive alternatives for economic well-being. It is valuable to analyze these examples of progressive change movements and to examine the congruence, or incongruence, of their strategies with social work values. It is also important to compare these examples with more specifically regressive social movements that have a powerful capacity to stall the gradual improvements in local to international social, economic, and environmental well-being to which community practitioners are committed.

For this work we identify advocacy, facilitation, and leadership as critical roles. In previous chapters of the workbook and in the *CPS* textbook, we propose practice strategies to strengthen skills related to these roles. In the following exercises our purpose is to deepen the critical thinking of community practice workers in preparation for engaging with progressive social movements. These exercises can also help to connect community practice workers with the broader efforts and networks across the globe working to strengthen progressive social movements.

INDIVIDUAL ASSESSMENT AND SMALL-GROUP DISCUSSION: WHAT MAKES SOCIAL MOVEMENTS PROGRESSIVE OR REGRESSIVE?

Identify a progressive social movement of which you are a member or would like to be a member. Explore the attributes of the movement that make it progressive (i.e., gradually moving toward improvement, especially in the areas of social, economic, and environmental well-being, social justice, and human rights). Determine how the specific movement is organized and how it is moving toward improvement. Important items to list would be the mission statement, the goals, the organizational inclusiveness, diverse support, the structure, and the global reach of the organization you select. Identify the values that form the basis for the movement's mission and compare them with social work values. Research the history in order to determine the origins of the movement. For example, what were the pushes and pulls that helped build awareness in society regarding the need for the movement? Name the early identity or interest groups that generated coalitions of groups to move in the same direction and form the beginnings of a social movement.

Now perform the same research and analysis for a social movement you believe is regressive (opposed to some aspects of social justice; not supportive of equal human rights). Identify the attributes that show that the movement tries to maintain the status quo or even retreat from policies that support inclusive social, economic, and environmental well-being. Research the history of the groups and organizations that provide leadership for the movement and explain the societal concerns that contributed to the impetus of the movement. What are the values that form the basis for the organizations that lead the movement toward what you consider a regressive position? Compare these values with social work values.

Share your discoveries with other members of your group to compare the progressive and regressive attributes of various social movements. Finally, imagine facilitating a discussion you have arranged with leaders of two opposing social movements. How would you best prepare for such facilitation? Write a brief statement or bullet points about how you would plan to facilitate such a discussion. Post all the statements in the classroom and review them to further explore strategies for facilitation.

CLASS OR SMALL-GROUP ACTIVITY: GRASSROOTS DEVELOPMENT TOWARD A SOCIAL MOVEMENT

Review the Millennium Development Goals from chapter 1 (CPS, p. 20), as well as the Save the Children UK "Call for Action" and the IFSW "Globalization Directive," both included in chapter 12 of CPS (p. 407). Given the economic downturn in the entire world's economies expected in the next several years, how could you help an organization frame a response to the significant needs of those people worldwide who are most economically vulnerable as outlined in these three documents? Can you identify several like-minded organizations that might frame a response to diminish the effects of a worldwide economic recession for the most vulnerable? Take the challenge!

- With your small group develop a strategy or strategies to respond to the basic needs of the most impoverished children and families in the world. In the guiding steps section of chapter 12 of *CPS*, we have listed seven levels of potential involvement drawn from Richard J. Estes's 1993 article, "Toward Sustainable Development: From Theory to Praxis" (*Social Development Issues* 15[3]: 1–29). Develop your set of strategies for only the first four levels: individual empowerment, conflict resolution, community building, and institution building.
- Now visit the WiserEarth Web site (http://www.wiserearth.org/) to find other organizations throughout the world with which your hypothetical social movement might link.

INDIVIDUAL EXERCISE AND SMALL-GROUP ACTIVITY: DRAWING FROM THE BENEFITS OF SOCIAL MOVEMENTS

The Self Employed Women's Association case example describes an organization that has benefited from the fruits of the labor movement, the cooperative movement, and the women's movement. If the ripples from these movements had not been pushing across the social and economic networks of the world in the last thirty years, the opportunity to establish such an organization may not have presented itself. Now SEWA, the Self Employed Women's Association in India, calls itself a social movement, stimulating women's awareness of their important role in the economy, demonstrating how their collaboration can benefit each of them as individuals, and how fairness in wages and work can be the subject of advocacy campaigns. SEWA, having blended the benefits of the cooperative, labor, and women's movements into their own special model for economic and social well-being, has exported its model to South Africa, Turkey, and Yemen.

SELF EMPLOYED WOMEN'S ASSOCIATION
PREPARED BY EMILY MACGUIRE

The Self Employed Women's Association (SEWA) was established as a trade union in December 1971 in support of self-employed women in India. Since its inception, SEWA has focused on two goals: full employment and self-reliance. The Association's

CONTINUED

members created an evaluation tool for these goals based on the following set of questions:

- Have more members obtained more employment?
- Has their income increased?
- Have they obtained food and nutrition?
- Has their health been safeguarded?
- Have they obtained child care?
- Have they obtained or improved their housing?
- Have their assets increased?
- Has the workers' organizational strength increased?
- Have workers' leadership activities and responsibilities increased?
- Have they become self-reliant both collectively and individually?
- Have they become literate?

The membership has maintained a steady rate of growth from 320 in 1973 to 959,689 in 2006. Since the 1980s, the focus of SEWA has broadened from its earlier urban focus to include organizing women in rural areas.

The organization works primarily with four types of self-employed women: vendors, home-based workers, manual laborers, and producers. The vendor category includes hawkers and women who sell fruits, vegetables, and other food items, as well as household items and clothes, in a market setting. Home-based workers are artisans such as weavers and potters, ready-made garment workers, and women who process agricultural products. The manual laborer group includes construction workers, contract laborers, handcart pullers, and domestic workers. Producers carry out their own businesses in activities such as cattle rearing and tree gum collecting.

Organizing rural workers has been on the SEWA agenda since 1979. The aim of the rural efforts initially focused on raising the minimum wage. Through this process, the organization became aware of the need to strengthen rural women's bargaining power and job opportunities. Since then, the rural organizing strategy has focused on increasing employment opportunities for women, working with rural women to develop leadership skills, and collaborating with existing rural development programs.

For SEWA, urban organizing has transformed over the years. At the beginning of the organization's history, many women in urban settings worked for the textile industry. Changes to the industry caused these women to lose their jobs to machines and move into the construction industry. The construction workers have organized to discuss the need for state labor protection laws and to demand laws that would protect workers in the industry. The workers have requested policy changes, including the development and implementation of social security services, accident insurance, and skill-based training.

SEWA offers services in support of self-employed women including child care, health care, and housing support. It has also developed a new program to train women to become videographers and video technicians. The cutting-edge video program is run by a team of self-employed women. The teams have produced more than 200 videos on a variety of subjects. These tapes are used at SEWA meetings and trainings, as well as at national film festivals. Recently, the organization obtained new equipment and registered as a communications cooperative. This move affords SEWA

CONTINUED

and its members the opportunity to expand media production and progress toward self-reliance.

SEWA is a strong proponent of investment in social capital development. Through the SEWA Academy, the organization encourages capacity building among its members. The SEWA Academy is the members' "university," which strives to build the organization's movement through developing the members' leadership skills and self-confidence. The learning process in this environment stresses sharing among leaders and members through small-group meetings and forums to share experiences and ideas. The Academy focuses on teaching about organizing, the women's movement, and SEWA's values through training, literacy work, research, and print and media communication activities.

The organization has explored the impacts of globalization on its membership. Its findings highlight three consequences of globalization: "a lagging behind of the productivity and wages of the unskilled as a result of global and national technical progress; an increased vulnerability and insecurity in the new market and trade oriented world, despite other benefits that these same trends have produced; and a decrease in the bargaining power of unskilled workers as a result of the greater mobility of capital and skilled labor." As a result, SEWA encourages women to deal with the changes brought about by globalization by taking advantage of new opportunities in the economy and resisting harmful changes, while advocating for policy changes for women in the informal sector.

SEWA developed four strategies to address the consequences of globalization:

- Organize membership-based associations of women.
- Build capacity with a focus on technical and managerial skills.
- Form capital in women's own names.
- Develop social security benefits.

The SEWA movement has a global presence, with organizations in South Africa, Turkey, and Yemen. In South Africa, the Self-Employed Women's Union (SEWU) is a union of informal sector workers. SEWA was instrumental in organizing the workers and continues to work closely with them on all informal sector issues and campaigns. SEWU has successfully advocated for vendors' rights and has made policy breakthroughs. Currently, SEWU is working with authorities in the city of Durban to include vendors' concerns in urban policies.

Source: Self Employed Women's Association. (2008). Retrieved February 11, 2008,
from http://www.sewa.org/index.asp.

SMALL-GROUP EXERCISE: COMPARING THE FOCUS OF RECENT SOCIAL MOVEMENTS

- Assign each person in your group one of the three movements from which SEWA benefited: the labor movement, the women's movement, and the cooperative movement. Have each member go to WiserEarth, or other international information sources you have available in print or via the Internet, and find an organization *on every continent in the world* that has benefited from the awareness stimulated by the labor movement, the women's movement, or the cooperative movement. If organizations have benefited from a combination of these movements, as has SEWA, all the better. List your findings, and make note of your responses to what you have found.

• Share your findings with each other in the small group. Imagine the world without the benefits stimulated by just these three progressive social and economic movements. How would members of your group like to see these movements progress? Write down members' ideas for future progress and share them with the class.

13

THE CHALLENGES FOR
COMMUNITY PRACTICE AHEAD

A s the old aphorism goes, "If you don't know where you are going, any path will do," which implies that you will have no idea of your destination along the way and may not recognize it when you arrive! An essential way to gain clarity about direction is to develop a clear and specific vision of needed change.

Visioning is a process that has long been practiced. Many Native American groups routinely used group visioning in relation to tribal plans and problem solving. If you can clarify your vision, you (individually or as a group) have a much greater chance of achieving desired goals—and can allow for flexibility and changes as you progress (Lee and Balkwill 1996; Chambers 2002).

VISION FOR A BETTER FUTURE: INDIVIDUAL AND GROUP EXERCISE

In this final chapter of the workbook, we ask that you engage in several types of visioning through creating your own and then a group vision of a better world, along with selecting strategies of community practice to achieve that vision. The last part of the chapter engages you in building a vision for your own development based on knowledge and skills audits and the creation of your own professional portfolio. Participating in these visioning processes, the self-audits, and the development of the portfolio can help prepare you to seek and find work that you love and to build a career based on your commitments.

INDIVIDUAL VISION (7 MINUTES)

- Individually write notes on large Post-its or half sheets of paper indicating important aspects of your own vision for a better world. Consider your own values, professional commitments, and the current challenges facing contemporary communities. On separate Post-its or half sheets, write down change strategies that you think can help to resolve or transform community problems.

CREATING A CLASS VISION STATEMENT USING CARDSTORMING (25 MINUTES)

- Divide the class into groups of 5 or 6 people. Share your individual vision ideas with members of your group. (At this point do not discuss change strategies.)
- Do round-robin discussion so that each person in the group presents one vision idea at a time. Go around the circle several times to gather ideas. Have a recorder write down all these initial vision ideas. Look for commonalities among the ideas and see if anyone has additional ideas to contribute.
- Review all the ideas; see if some of them combine effectively. Begin to create your shared vision of what you want to see in the world—particularly with regard to human rights and social justice.
- See if the group's ideas coalesce into several statements that everyone supports, and select the statements and ideas that you want to share with the class. (Ideas not yet incorporated may be added to the larger class vision later.)
- Use the Cardstorming process presented in chapter 5 of this book and post each group's selected ideas or sentences on a wall where everyone can see them.

After all group vision ideas are posted on the wall, everyone should come close enough to easily read all the notes. Select two class members to organize the notes into categories following instructions from class members so that categories are formed of related ideas. After all the Post-its are organized, name the categories that have been created.

- Divide into your small groups. The instructor or facilitator will assign each group one vision category to work on. Work together for 15 minutes to create the specific vision statement for that category.
- Each group will post their vision under the label for their category. One member of each group will read their group's component of the emerging class vision statement.
- As a full group discuss the vision statement components. Do the statements relate to each other? Do group members perceive any order or ways to connect the component statements into a whole?

Divide the class into two groups. One group will work on refining the class's work to make a clear and powerful vision statement.

The other group will combine their earlier thinking and work together to develop statements about change strategies that they will recommend as ways to achieve the goals inherent in the class vision statement. The group should list recommended strategies on easel paper and be prepared to discuss how the recommended strategies relate to components of the vision.

To conclude the exercise the "vision" group will write the revised Class Vision Statement on a chalkboard, a white board, or a banner of easel paper for final review.

The "change strategy" group will organize and list their recommended strategies to achieve the vision on easel paper. The class will conclude with discussion about how to apply the strategies for transformative social change.

INDIVIDUAL ACTIVITY: PERSONAL KNOWLEDGE AND SKILL SETS AUDITS

HOW TO KNOW "WHAT YOU KNOW": PROFESSIONAL DEVELOPMENT AND KNOWLEDGE

This final chapter of the CPS workbook concludes with assisting you in developing a professional portfolio to document and illustrate the skills and abilities you bring to your work. In preparation for the portfolio, we suggest two exercises to "audit" your present level of knowledge and skill development.

The two lists here provide a format for a "working audit" of your professional development in specific knowledge and skills areas. The first list notes core knowledge or areas of understanding that would be essential for successful community practice at the graduate level. The second list presents the skill sets we have identified in the CPS textbook as essential for successful work in the Eight Models of Community Practice described.

Although knowledge and skills are basic, they are not necessarily sufficient for good practice. In addition to the knowledge and skills necessary for community practice, one must work from an ethical base and have good judgment and the strength to be resilient in the face of setbacks and challenges. This working combination of knowledge, skills, judgment, ethics, and resilience is referred to as *competence*. For your portfolio and more importantly, in your practice, it will be important to focus your professional development so that over time you will attain the full range of competencies in your areas of specialization.

**CORE KNOWLEDGE AREAS FOR WORK IN COMMUNITY ORGANIZATION
AND SOCIAL ADMINISTRATION WITH A FOCUS ON ORGANIZING,
PLANNING, COLLABORATION, SUSTAINABLE DEVELOPMENT,
AND PROGRESSIVE CHANGE**
DOROTHY N. GAMBLE, IN COLLABORATION WITH MEMBERS OF ACOSA

In this core knowledge assessment, rate your present knowledge level from 1 to 5 (i.e.,
1 being inadequate and 5 being fully adequate). Following the rating, make notes that
suggest where or how you will gain more knowledge for that area (e.g., courses and
training, work and volunteer experience, etc.). Check your audit at least twice a year to
see how your level of knowledge and understanding has increased and where you may
need additional focus. You may also add some areas of knowledge as your professional
life develops and you go beyond the level expected for graduate students and into more
specific practice roles.

I. Organizing

    A. Knowledge for Organizing Services and Programs for Communities

        1. The comparative use of different organizational structures to accomplish hu-
           man services objectives (e.g., public institutions, community-based advocacy
           and service organizations, private organizations, public-private collaborations,
           cooperative services, etc.) to attain outcomes that improve the well-being of
           individuals, groups, families, and communities

           SELF-RATING   ACTION STEPS TO STRENGTHEN KNOWLEDGE

        2. The origins, context, and auspices of public and nonprofit human services or-
           ganizations as they seek to develop comprehensive community social and
           economic programs

           SELF-RATING   ACTION STEPS TO STRENGTHEN KNOWLEDGE

        3. Legislation, policies, and regulations that create and monitor public and
           nonprofit organizations, along with knowledge regarding legislative change,
           policy advocacy, and public civic education to promote equality and human
           rights

           SELF-RATING   ACTION STEPS TO STRENGTHEN KNOWLEDGE

CONTINUED

4. The range of public and private funding sources available for human services and community-based organizations and knowledge regarding proposal preparation and project financing

SELF-RATING   **ACTION STEPS TO STRENGTHEN KNOWLEDGE**
_____   _____

5. The leadership knowledge necessary for program design and implementation, managing and directing, staffing, financial management and budgeting, and monitoring and evaluating human services and community-based organizations

SELF-RATING   **ACTION STEPS TO STRENGTHEN KNOWLEDGE**
_____   _____

B. Knowledge for Organizing Community Groups

1. The comparative characteristics of different models for organizing communities (e.g., Eight Models of Community Practice), especially the potential for these models to empower communities, promote participation, and advocate for improved social, economic, and environmental well-being

SELF-RATING   **ACTION STEPS TO STRENGTHEN KNOWLEDGE**
_____   _____

2. Appropriate, effective, and ethical professional roles in working with community groups and organizations

SELF-RATING   **ACTION STEPS TO STRENGTHEN KNOWLEDGE**
_____   _____

3. The use and value of diversity (class, gender, race, culture, age, sexual preference, etc.) when facilitating the development of community groups

SELF-RATING   **ACTION STEPS TO STRENGTHEN KNOWLEDGE**
_____   _____

4. The functions of conflict, the value of difference, and the use of mediation and dialogue when working with community groups and coalitions

SELF-RATING   **ACTION STEPS TO STRENGTHEN KNOWLEDGE**
_____   _____

CONTINUED

5. The use of directed analytical discussion, information-linking techniques, democratic decision-making methods, and participatory education to strengthen the capacities of community groups and coalitions

SELF-RATING   **ACTION STEPS TO STRENGTHEN KNOWLEDGE**
_____   _____

II. Planning

A. Knowledge for Planning, Monitoring, and Evaluating Inclusive Human Service and Community Programs

1. The need for critical assessment and use of diverse sources of knowledge to prevent and diminish social, economic, and environmental problems and to promote social and economic progress and flourishing communities

SELF-RATING   **ACTION STEPS TO STRENGTHEN KNOWLEDGE**
_____   _____

2. The range of fact-finding and assessment tools and methods available to map assets and barriers to optimum emotional, social, and economic functioning of people

SELF-RATING   **ACTION STEPS TO STRENGTHEN KNOWLEDGE**
_____   _____

3. The need for clear mission and goal statements, consensus on desired outcomes, measurable evaluation criteria, and structures for monitoring progress in human service delivery and community program implementation

SELF-RATING   **ACTION STEPS TO STRENGTHEN KNOWLEDGE**
_____   _____

4. The broad range of quantitative and qualitative research methods available, including participatory research and self-evaluation, for evaluating programs and services

SELF-RATING   **ACTION STEPS TO STRENGTHEN KNOWLEDGE**
_____   _____

5. The role that political environments, economic conditions, and cultural/racial/gender intolerance play in influencing human service, community program planning, and research activities, along with strategies to influence planning and research that embrace diversity

SELF-RATING   **ACTION STEPS TO STRENGTHEN KNOWLEDGE**
_____   _____

CONTINUED

B. <u>Knowledge for Planning, Monitoring, and Evaluating Community Development Strategies</u>

1. The need for critical assessment and use of diverse sources of knowledge to facilitate effective development of social, economic, and environmental programs

SELF-RATING   ACTION STEPS TO STRENGTHEN KNOWLEDGE

2. The role of "expert knowledge" that community members bring to the planning processes, and skills to be able to access local and indigenous knowledge

SELF-RATING   ACTION STEPS TO STRENGTHEN KNOWLEDGE

3. The ways to facilitate consensus building and effective decision making so that clear mission, goals, and evaluation statements can be established in community groups and coalitions

SELF-RATING   ACTION STEPS TO STRENGTHEN KNOWLEDGE

4. The value of information exchange and peer learning in helping community groups network with like-minded organizations

SELF-RATING   ACTION STEPS TO STRENGTHEN KNOWLEDGE

5. The role that political environments, economic conditions, and cultural/racial/gender intolerance play in influencing community planning and priority-setting activities and methods to promote multicultural learning, intergroup relations, and community collaborations

SELF-RATING   ACTION STEPS TO STRENGTHEN KNOWLEDGE

III. Collaboration

A. <u>Knowledge of Strategies for Collaboration among Nonprofit, Public, and Private Organizations</u>

1. Social work's value base and its congruence with various strategies for improving social, economic, and environmental well-being through building relationships based in equality, opportunity, advocacy, mutuality, humility, and community

SELF-RATING   ACTION STEPS TO STRENGTHEN KNOWLEDGE

CONTINUED

2. The forces that prevent progressive solutions to community problems and the need for broad collaborative efforts to launch campaigns for policy and program changes

SELF-RATING   **ACTION STEPS TO STRENGTHEN KNOWLEDGE**

3. The factors and conditions that facilitate the coming together of different organizations for a common purpose that will improve social, economic, and environmental well-being

SELF-RATING   **ACTION STEPS TO STRENGTHEN KNOWLEDGE**

4. The range of networking, facilitative, and technical skills needed for collaborative efforts (e.g., task group facilitation, decision making, team building, conflict management, culture/racial/gender-sensitive organizational structures, ethical audits, electronic and standard communication, dialogue and mediation, etc.)

SELF-RATING   **ACTION STEPS TO STRENGTHEN KNOWLEDGE**

5. The knowledge and skills needed to connect service consumers and community members with any organizational collaborative using empowerment principles

SELF-RATING   **ACTION STEPS TO STRENGTHEN KNOWLEDGE**

B. Knowledge of Strategies for Collaboration among Identity and Interest Groups

1. Mapping the depth, breadth, and diversity of community groups, and facilitating their collaboration with groups that have similar goals and outcome objectives

SELF-RATING   **ACTION STEPS TO STRENGTHEN KNOWLEDGE**

2. Facilitating decision making, problem solving, and priority setting in a range of groups from small task groups to large community coalitions

SELF-RATING   **ACTION STEPS TO STRENGTHEN KNOWLEDGE**

CONTINUED

3. The importance of celebrations, marking of milestones, and recognition of hard work in all community-wide efforts

SELF-RATING   **ACTION STEPS TO STRENGTHEN KNOWLEDGE**

4. The value and importance of peer learning in community-wide collaboratives for social change

SELF-RATING   **ACTION STEPS TO STRENGTHEN KNOWLEDGE**

5. Methods for strengthening leadership and organizational capacity in grassroots groups

SELF-RATING   **ACTION STEPS TO STRENGTHEN KNOWLEDGE**

IV. Development

A. Knowledge for Organizational Development

1. The comparative roles of public, nonprofit, and proprietary organizations in providing human services and community programs to people

SELF-RATING   **ACTION STEPS TO STRENGTHEN KNOWLEDGE**

2. Organizational and systems theories and their use in organizational assessment and organizational development

SELF-RATING   **ACTION STEPS TO STRENGTHEN KNOWLEDGE**

3. The range of leadership and management knowledge necessary to facilitate the effective functioning of human services and community-based organizations

SELF-RATING   **ACTION STEPS TO STRENGTHEN KNOWLEDGE**

4. The role of missions, goals, auspices, structure, human and material resources, formal and informal culture, and outcomes in assessing the effective functioning of organizations

SELF-RATING   **ACTION STEPS TO STRENGTHEN KNOWLEDGE**

CONTINUED

5. The application of social work values, especially social justice, human rights, integrity, and competence, in developing effective human service and community-based organizations

SELF-RATING   **ACTION STEPS TO STRENGTHEN KNOWLEDGE**

B. Knowledge for Community Social, Economic, and Sustainable Development

1. The range of human development indicators, including those developed by the United Nations Development Program, and specific community sustainable development indicators now available in many communities to measure social, economic, and environmental well-being

SELF-RATING   **ACTION STEPS TO STRENGTHEN KNOWLEDGE**

2. The linkages between effective family functioning and strong, integrated community institutions for improving the general social, economic, and environmental well-being of people in a community

SELF-RATING   **ACTION STEPS TO STRENGTHEN KNOWLEDGE**

3. The range of resources necessary in any community for effective human development (e.g., education, health promotion, housing, leisure, and spiritual resources, along with work opportunities, transportation, and protection from violence, natural disasters, and environmental decline, etc.)

SELF-RATING   **ACTION STEPS TO STRENGTHEN KNOWLEDGE**

4. The conditions, especially those related to gender bias and racial prejudice, that make these resources inaccessible for some community members and knowledge of methods to promote inclusion

SELF-RATING   **ACTION STEPS TO STRENGTHEN KNOWLEDGE**

5. The broad range of social and economic programs employed in the developing world (e.g., microenterprise, community banking models, cooperative and solidarity production models) that can be adapted for local communities anywhere, including in the United States

SELF-RATING   **ACTION STEPS TO STRENGTHEN KNOWLEDGE**

CONTINUED

V. Change: Advocacy, Policy Practice, Social Justice, and Human Rights

A. Knowledge of Organizational and Community Change for Social Justice and Human Rights

1. The basic human rights documents, conventions, and covenants accepted by the international community that serve as guides to working toward improved social, economic, and environmental well-being (available on IFSW Web site)

   SELF-RATING   ACTION STEPS TO STRENGTHEN KNOWLEDGE

2. The value of participatory processes for identifying issues, defining strategies, organizing campaigns for change, and evaluating outcomes

   SELF-RATING   ACTION STEPS TO STRENGTHEN KNOWLEDGE

3. The political process and how to assess the political climate for engaging in organizational and community change

   SELF-RATING   ACTION STEPS TO STRENGTHEN KNOWLEDGE

4. Analyzing the context and engaging the key actors and institutions necessary for providing leadership and support in an organizational or community change process

   SELF-RATING   ACTION STEPS TO STRENGTHEN KNOWLEDGE

5. Practice principles that will increase empowerment among organizations and community members who have been most excluded from decision-making and policy-making circles

   SELF-RATING   ACTION STEPS TO STRENGTHEN KNOWLEDGE

B. Knowledge of Policy Practice Principles Necessary for Improving Social, Economic, and Environmental Well-being

1. The significance of advocacy and empowerment in the history of social work practice and knowledge of historical role models for this work

   SELF-RATING   ACTION STEPS TO STRENGTHEN KNOWLEDGE

CONTINUED

2. The functioning of human services policy-making arenas including organizations, municipalities, county governments, state legislatures, the Congress, executive branches, and the courts, and how to access them

SELF-RATING **ACTION STEPS TO STRENGTHEN KNOWLEDGE**

3. Knowledge and skills involved in negotiation, mediation, and reframing in working for organizational and community change

SELF-RATING **ACTION STEPS TO STRENGTHEN KNOWLEDGE**

4. Knowledge and skills needed to develop effective public communication and lobbying efforts, especially the use of electronic technology for accessing and disseminating information generated from policy analysis

SELF-RATING **ACTION STEPS TO STRENGTHEN KNOWLEDGE**

5. Social work organizations and coalitions engaged in effective policy change at local, regional, national, and international levels

SELF-RATING **ACTION STEPS TO STRENGTHEN KNOWLEDGE**

COMMUNITY PRACTICE SKILLS AUDIT

Gamble and Weil have identified specific skills that are critical in each of the eight models described in the *CPS* text. Although linked with specific chapters, some of the skills are important in multiple models of practice and should be considered overall. Continue a self-audit in the following table, considering not only how effectively you are able to master the skills, but also how you might be able to teach, coach, train, and facilitate community leaders as they work to develop these skills. As in the previous knowledge audit, rate your present skill level from 1 to 5 (i.e., 1 being inadequate, 5 being fully adequate). Following the rating, make notes that suggest where or how you will gain skills for that area (e.g., courses and training, work and volunteer experience, etc.). Check your audit at least twice a year to see how your level of skills has increased and where you may need additional focus. You may also add some skills areas as your professional life develops and you go beyond the level expected for graduate students and into more specific practice roles.

COMMUNITY PRACTICE SKILLS AUDIT:
SUMMARY OF SKILLS IDENTIFIED AS CRITICAL IN CHAPTERS 5–13 OF *COMMUNITY*
PRACTICE SKILLS: LOCAL TO GLOBAL PERSPECTIVES

CHAPTER 5 SKILL SETS FOR NEIGHBORHOOD AND COMMUNITY ORGANIZING	CURRENT RATING	ACTION STEPS TO STRENGTHEN SKILLS
Culturally sensitive engagement with community members and groups and the practice of active listening		
Effective group facilitation and engaging groups in dialogue		
Teaching decision-making techniques		
Conducting mediation		
Engaging groups in planning for action		

CHAPTER 6 SKILL SETS FOR ORGANIZING FUNCTIONAL COMMUNITIES	CURRENT RATING	ACTION STEPS TO STRENGTHEN SKILLS
Using a framework to apply human rights and social justice principles to social problem analysis (e.g., Finn and Jacobson 2008; Cohen, de la Vega, and Watson 2001; VeneKlasen and Miller 2002)		
Serving as an advocate and coaching/training others to be advocates on their own behalf		
Effectively speaking and writing as an advocate for social justice and human rights		

CONTINUED

CHAPTER 6 SKILL SETS FOR ORGANIZING FUNCTIONAL COMMUNITIES	CURRENT RATING	ACTION STEPS TO STRENGTHEN SKILLS
Building leadership and networking skills in community groups		

CHAPTER 7 SKILL SETS FOR SOCIAL, ECONOMIC, AND SUSTAINABLE DEVELOPMENT	CURRENT RATING	ACTION STEPS TO STRENGTHEN SKILLS
Application of human rights and social justice principles to identify basic human needs (e.g., drawing from Jim Ife; Elizabeth Reichert; UN Development Programs *Human Development Reports*, etc.)		
Combining social, economic, and environmental well-being in the analysis of community development progress		
Facilitating the development of community sustainability outcome measures (e.g., drawing from Maureen Hart and others)		

CHAPTER 8 SKILL SETS FOR INCLUSIVE PROGRAM DEVELOPMENT	CURRENT RATING	ACTION STEPS TO STRENGTHEN SKILLS
Gaining entry into a community by listening and learning from members; asking questions; being congruent and authentic in your interactions and communications; and explaining your interest in mutual work with them on issues of their concern		
Applying and teaching critical thinking skills in analysis of issues and analysis and synthesis of ideas for program development		
Making ethical decisions with regard to your responsibilities and		

CONTINUED

CHAPTER 8 SKILL SETS FOR INCLUSIVE PROGRAM DEVELOPMENT	CURRENT RATING	ACTION STEPS TO STRENGTHEN SKILLS
interactions with community members and others, and assisting groups in analyzing ethical dilemmas in community engagement and program design		
Conducting and coaching visioning exercises with groups to assist them in recognizing and finding consensus on desired future states		
Using and teaching communication skills for mutual problem solving and program planning		
Acting as a spokesperson when necessary to advocate for community groups and progressive responses to community needs; coaching members in self-advocacy		
Using and teaching methods to assess needs and interests (assessment evaluation) in possible community-based programs, and program evaluation		

CHAPTER 9 SKILL SETS FOR COMMUNITIES AND SOCIAL PLANNING	CURRENT RATING	ACTION STEPS TO STRENGTHEN SKILLS
Engaging with community members and groups to initiate a process of neighborhood planning that is based in their ideas, knowledge, and concerns		
Using and teaching communication methods (written and oral) that will clarify technical tasks, support mutual work, and assist in community-based planning and decision making		

CONTINUED

CHAPTER 9 SKILL SETS FOR COMMUNITIES AND SOCIAL PLANNING	CURRENT RATING	ACTION STEPS TO STRENGTHEN SKILLS
Facilitating group interactions in complex planning processes and between community members and external organizations with whom they need to work		
Managing the process of inclusive planning; ensuring that diverse positions are heard and that groups work together effectively; assigning, coordinating, and monitoring task accomplishment to move plans forward		
Teaching participatory research methods and using existing research and outcomes of other planning efforts to assist local work		
Assembling and using social indicator data; working with community groups to assess the impact of social indicators and add updated information to give a clearer picture of community conditions		
Participatory planning—preparing multiple, diverse community groups to use methods of participatory planning to assess issues, develop community improvement plans, and monitor and evaluate planning processes		
Performing process and outcome evaluations using multiple quantitative and qualitative methods to determine outcomes of social planning projects		
Developing proposals funding and seeking resources for community		

CONTINUED

CHAPTER 9 SKILL SETS FOR COMMUNITIES AND SOCIAL PLANNING	CURRENT RATING	ACTION STEPS TO STRENGTHEN SKILLS
programs and projects; teaching and coaching community members on technical tasks and proposal preparation, and on acting as spokespersons for proposals when they are reviewed		
Encouraging consumer and community participation in all stages of local planning		

CHAPTER 10 SKILL SETS FOR BUILDING EFFECTIVE COALITIONS	CURRENT RATING	ACTION STEPS TO STRENGTHEN SKILLS
Effective engagement with collaborative groups to develop advocacy plans		
Engagement with collaborative groups to assist in the effective management of their mission, goals, outcome objectives, and action strategies		
Effective use of direct practice skills to strengthen the leadership and participation capacities of coalition members		
Effective use of community organizing skills to build a strong coalition		
Application of social justice, cultural sensitivity, and participatory methods in all of the above skills		

CHAPTER 11 SKILL SETS FOR POLITICAL AND SOCIAL ACTION	CURRENT RATING	ACTION STEPS TO STRENGTHEN SKILLS
Effectively organize and coordinate political and social action groups		

CONTINUED

CHAPTER 11 SKILL SETS FOR POLITICAL AND SOCIAL ACTION	CURRENT RATING	ACTION STEPS TO STRENGTHEN SKILLS
Engage with action groups to analyze the effects of local, regional, national, and international policies on the economic, social, and environmental conditions of people		
Engage with community members to identify social, economic, and environmental well-being indicators for *all* sectors of the community		
Effectively advocate for improving social, economic, and environmental well-being, especially for the most vulnerable populations		

CHAPTER 12 SKILL SETS FOR MOVEMENTS FOR PROGRESSIVE CHANGE	CURRENT RATING	ACTION STEPS TO STRENGTHEN SKILLS
Active participation and collaboration with progressive social movements in their efforts to build effective networks		
Effective facilitation of consensus building and goal attainment in work with social movements		
Effective leadership in the development of networks and collaborations for progressive social movements		

CHAPTER 13 SKILL SETS	CURRENT RATING	ACTION STEPS TO STRENGTHEN SKILLS
Visioning and leading visioning exercises		
Developing, using, and teaching self-auditing and program/project auditing tools		
Portfolio preparation		

We hope these self-audits of knowledge and skills are useful to remind you of your own knowledge base, the skills you have mastered, and the action steps you will take to build advanced knowledge and skills in these and other skills areas that emerge as you move through your career in community practice.

PERSONAL EXPERIENCE AND VISION: DOCUMENTING YOUR SKILLS AND CHARTING YOUR COURSE— CREATING YOUR PORTFOLIO

Increasingly, students and professionals are expected to have a *professional portfolio* that documents their preparation, skills, knowledge, and accomplishments. A portfolio may be particularly useful to you in pursuing your first post–master's degree job. The portfolio preparation ideas presented next were adapted from a PowerPoint presentation by Sarah Axelson (2008) for students graduating from the UNC–Chapel Hill School of Social Work. For this publication, additional information and examples have been added by Marie Weil. We hope this guide will be useful to you in clarifying your vision for your career and for developing your own portfolio.

CREATING A PROFESSIONAL PORTFOLIO
SARAH AXELSON, ADVOCATES FOR YOUTH, WASHINGTON, D.C., AND MARIE WEIL, UNC–CHAPEL HILL SCHOOL OF SOCIAL WORK

You might question your own need for a portfolio, or even wonder what one is since we most typically think of artists carrying a portfolio of their creative work. Your portfolio will do much the same; essentially, a *professional portfolio* for community practitioners is a collection of documents, information, and materials that provides visible evidence of your experience and accomplishments. It presents information about you and provides illustrations of your work. Your portfolio will help potential employers get to know you and understand your interests and abilities through perusal of the materials as well as talking with you during your interviews.

A portfolio will provide you with a dynamic, long-term tool that can help you organize information about yourself and communicate effectively with potential employers. When you know that you are prepared to present your strongest professional abilities along with a clear "picture" of who you are, you can be more relaxed in interview situations.

Critically, your portfolio assists you in guiding job interviews to allow you to discuss your skills, experience, and interests so that you are more "in charge" of the interview and can be more confident that you will have the opportunity to discuss your strengths and frame your discussion so that the potential employer understands you as a professional and a person.

CONTINUED

If you wonder what difference a portfolio will make for you as you launch your career in community practice, consider the following:

1. A portfolio provides proof of your preparation and previous work, your professional experience, educational experience, and special skills and abilities.
2. It can give you an edge in job seeking—you are well prepared for interviews with written documents and exhibits. In addition, creating the portfolio engages you in a useful process of reflection.
3. You can gain something from the process—collecting your materials and reflecting on where you have been and where you want to go will confirm your knowledge and skills, and deepen your perspective about your work and career direction.

Why not develop a portfolio? It is relatively painless, and it may be of considerable benefit. The following discussion provides information on formats and materials typically included in portfolios, and how to create and use your own portfolio.

PREPARING YOUR PORTFOLIO
Formats

You may choose to develop a hard-copy portfolio or an electronic version. Each approach has its advantages:

HARD COPY

Advantage—easy to share in interviews
—three-ring binder
—paper copies of all materials
—controlled distribution
—good reference during interviews
—faster to make changes for different job interviews

ELECTRONIC

Availability to review
—good for follow-up
—password protection optional
—extended review time
—demonstrates technological literacy

What Does a Portfolio Include?

Use any combination of the following tabbed sections:

Table of Contents	Work Philosophy
Career Goals	Resume
Work Samples	Community Service
Awards and Achievements	References
Statement of Originality	

CONTINUED

Work Philosophy

This is a personal statement about yourself and your work orientation; it can include:

- Your values for practice;
- Your perspective and reasons for wanting to work with groups, communities, and organizations (why community practice is important to you);
- Your perspective on professional behavior in organizations and communities;
- Your sense of the type of organizational culture within which you hope to work;
- Your sense of how to facilitate work and task accomplishment in diverse groups within communities and organizations;
- Your sense of professional responsibilities to others—the people you serve, colleagues, and community organizations;
- The ultimate goals that you want to strive for in your career.

In your statement of your work philosophy, think carefully about what you want to say. Be sure to place your most central values and beliefs first; and have a colleague or friend review it for cogency and clarity. This is your place to make a personal statement, and it should reflect who you are—your goals and direction—without, however, becoming too personal.

SAMPLE STATEMENTS—REVIEW THESE STATEMENTS AND WRITE TWO STATEMENTS FOR YOURSELF

Long-term, sustainable change can only be achieved when community members, consumer groups, and clients have the opportunity to participate in the decisions that affect their lives.

Your Turn:

The organization's mission should be lived out in daily operations and reflected in the organizational culture. The mission should guide decision-making processes in work with program participants, community members, and colleagues.

Your Turn:

Where Do You Want to Be in Two Years? in Five Years?

Take a few minutes to write a brief list of ideas about where you want to be professionally in two and in five years. For example: What types of communities and groups do you want to work with? What social issues and community concerns are of greatest interest to you? What kind of work setting is most appealing? What type of work do you want to be doing? This reflection will help you draft more specific career goals.

CAREER GOALS

- Set a direction for your career and briefly describe it.
- State experiences you have had that build on this direction.

CONTINUED

- Provide information about the professional achievements you want to accomplish and the knowledge and skills you want to acquire.
- Tips
  - Present two- and five-year goals.
  - Be sure that some, if not all, goals are measurable.

SAMPLE GOALS AND YOUR GOALS

TWO-YEAR GOAL	YOUR TURN: TWO-YEAR GOAL(S)

To strengthen my training skills by:

Taking a short course.

Shadowing a colleague who is an expert trainer in multiple training sessions.
Preparing and presenting three different training courses twice each within two years.

YOUR TURN: FIVE-YEAR GOAL(S)	YOUR TURN: FIVE-YEAR GOAL(S)

Resumes and Resume Writing

A resume is the document that presents your work and academic experience, together with other relevant information that you want potential employers to know about you. Very likely there are faculty members or advisers at your college or university who can advise you about resume preparation and style.

Essentially, it is important for a resume to be well organized, easily readable, and brief enough that potential employers will take the time to review it. Pay careful attention to format and "readability." Your resume is often the first information a possible employer will have about you, and it needs to be carefully constructed. Be mindful that many potential employers now review Facebook, MySpace, and other online information sources. Be sure that you do not post materials in such sites that you would not want a potential employer to see. Resumes will differ in style and content related to the amount of relevant work experience writers have. Remember that whether you have years of experience or are relatively less experienced, your job is to present your combination of experience, education, capabilities, interests, and additional information so that it catches the attention and interest of reviewers.

Although resumes are rather structured and formal (or "cut and dried") in their appearance, you also have the responsibility to write an application letter tailored to each

CONTINUED

job for which you apply. Specificity in your letters will help you be persuasive about your abilities, your commitment to community practice, and your suitability for the particular position. The following format is fairly typical for resumes:

YOUR NAME
YOUR ADDRESS, PHONE, E-MAIL (WEB SITE IF APPLICABLE)

Education: most recent first	Degree(s)	Place(s)
Special Training: most recent first	Topics	Where and When

Professional Experience:
  (this can include your internships) most recent first

Employment [List most recent first and provide the information needed for each subheading for each position you have held (including internships and meaningful volunteer experiences)]:
  For each job position or internship specify the following points:

Dates of Employment

Organization—Name and Address

Title of Your Job

Major Responsibilities

Presentations Given:

Trainings Conducted:

Certificates Earned and Trainings Attended:

Skills:

Interests:

Work Samples

This is the major portion of the portfolio and the most powerful part of your presentation—select your best materials.

- Common sources of work samples (emphasize your interests and strengths)
  - Classroom projects, papers, PowerPoints, report summaries—consider practice, policy, and research course materials
  - Materials from your internships and previous jobs
  - Summaries and documentary materials from community service projects

CONTINUED

- Tips
  - Start saving your work today! Customize the work samples you present in interviews to match the job description and interview focus.
  - For longer materials include a summary; offer the full product.

Possible Work Samples

You might include:

- Flyers from trainings you have conducted
- The flyer or announcement of a community education program you offered
- Reports on social problems you have written for your field practice agency
- A copy of a real or simulated proposal for funding or selected materials
- Information about programs you have helped to develop
- List of major responsibilities/accomplishments in your internships
- Copies of your best academic papers and projects—consider ways to include materials related to practice, policy, and research classes.

Awards, Achievements, and Memberships

If you have received special recognitions, list them here, and be sure to provide documentation of any awards you have received, such as:

- Scholarships
- College, university, or school awards
- Community or public service recognitions
- Agency recognitions
- Membership in professional organizations
- Special certificates
- Recognition from professional group

Place the most recent items first and be selective—a short list here is not a problem.

Community Service and Volunteer Experience

Community service and volunteering are important and send a very positive message about your interests and commitments. This section can include volunteer efforts in your school as well as service in the community.

- Tips
  - Choose causes/activities you are proud of.
  - Keep your samples up to date.
  - Don't underestimate the importance of this section of your portfolio.

References

Written, telephone, or e-mail references will provide additional insight into your skills, professionalism, and commitments.

CONTINUED

TIPS:

> Select the people who will be your references carefully. It is valuable to have at least one faculty member; your supervisor, manager, or director from your internship; and your supervisor from previous work experience (or significant volunteer experience).
> Give the people who will write your references guidance about what topics it will be important to cover in their letters. What aspects of their knowledge about you will be most important? You might also provide a note with a few bullet points about what you hope they will cover.

Sample Statement of Originality

"This portfolio is the work of [*your name*]. Please do not copy without permission. Some of the exhibits, work samples, and/or service samples are the proprietary property of the organization whose name appears on the document. Each has granted permission for this product to be used as a demonstration of my work, and portfolio material is not to be used for any other purposes."

IN CREATING YOUR PORTFOLIO

> A little planning goes a long way!
> Save all the project material and papers you create.
> Collect and organize your work samples.
> Draft material that needs to be written up.
> Pull it all together—in a well-organized and visually appealing format.

WHEN SHOULD YOU USE YOUR PORTFOLIO?

- Tips for Interviewing:
  - Refer to and point out a document or information from your portfolio at least once or twice in the first 15 minutes.
  - Overview your work philosophy and professional goals (turn to them in the portfolio and state a couple of points as highlights)
  - Point out your resume—you might also note particular training, work, or educational experiences that are relevant for the particular position.
  - Describe briefly what each section entails.
- Follow-up Interviews: When interviewing for community practice positions, you may find that you will be asked or expected to participate in one or more group interviews and/or sequential interviews with different organization members.
  - For a Group Interview: It can be useful to ask if there will be one—so you can be prepared! For a group interview, you might bring two copies of your portfolio as well as additional copies of your resume. With a group interview, be sure that you address each person and seek their participation; and if not everyone has access to your materials, be sure that you present the central points you want to make verbally to all interview participants.

CONTINUED

- For Sequential Interviews: Be sure that you carry your portfolio from room to room and select the most pertinent information to share with each person who interviews you. For example, a program manager, a project director, and the executive director might each be interested in some different aspects of your experience.
- Performance Reviews: Be sure to keep your portfolio up to date in your current job. It can be very useful in updating your program director or executive director about your special projects and accomplishments over the past year. It can be especially useful to provide illustrations about how your work has contributed to overall agency mission and goals.

Maximizing the Use of Your Portfolio in Interviews: The Initial Answer to Many Questions Is—

"Well, that is highlighted in my portfolio . . ."

SAMPLE INTERVIEWER QUESTIONS

What are your five-year career goals?
What do you do for recreation?
   (Consider community service.)
What was your most difficult project?
   (Refer to your work samples.)
What certifications do you hold?
What special training have you taken?
   (Refer to resume or achievements.)

Each of these areas is highlighted in your portfolio.

For additional information you may consult the following Web sites for examples of E-portfolios:

- http://www.eportfolio.psu.edu/
- University of Washington—graduate program in nutrition example, http://portfolio.washington.edu/nutr/ns-graduate-portfolio/221300.html
- San Francisco State-Department of Health Education MPH Portfolio example, http://www.sfsu.edu/~hed/masters/portfolio.htm

The portfolio should be useful in your planning, and we wish you good luck in your career development.

CONCLUDING NOTE

We hope that the CPS textbook and accompanying workbook have provided support for you in at least two ways:

CONTINUED

1. Increasing your confidence in applying practice judgments and ethics; and
2. Assisting you in making major progress in developing and integrating knowledge and skills for compassionate and effective community practice.

With strengthened confidence, knowledge, and skills, your resilience—even in tough practice situations—should increase, preparing you for ongoing work and additional challenges in community practice.

REFERENCES

Axelson, Sarah. February 2008. *Preparing Your Portfolio.* A PowerPoint slide show presented at the School of Social Work, University of North Carolina, Chapel Hill.

Chambers, Robert. 1997. *Whose Reality Counts? Putting the First Last.* London: Intermediate Technology Publications.

Chambers, Robert. 2002. *Participatory Workshops: A Sourcebook of 21 Sets of Ideas and Activities.* Sterling, VA: Earthscan Publications.

Cohen, David, Rosa de la Vega, and Gabrielle Watson. 2001. *Advocacy for Social Justice: A Global Action and Reflection Guide.* Bloomfield, CT: Kumarian Press.

Finn, Janet L., and Maxine Jacobson. 2008. *Just Practice: A Social Justice Approach to Social Work*, 2nd ed. Peosta, IA: Eddie Bowers Publishing.

Hart, Maureen. 1999. *Guide to Sustainable Community Indicators*, 2nd ed. North Andover, MA: Hart Environmental Data. Retrieved February 8, 2008, from http://www.sustainablemeasures.com/.

Ife, Jim. 2007. October. "The New International Agendas: What Role for Social Work." Hokenstad International Social Work Lecture, Council on Social Work Education, San Francisco, California.

Ife, Jim. 2008. *Human Rights and Social Work: Toward Rights-Based Practice.* Rev. ed. Cambridge, UK: Cambridge University Press.

Lee, Bill, and Mike Balkwill. 1996. *Participatory Planning for Action.* Toronto, Ontario: Commonact Press.

Reichert, Elizabeth, ed. 2007. *Challenges in Human Rights: A Social Work Perspective.* New York: Columbia University Press.

United Nations Development Programme (UNDP). 2007. *Human Development Report 2007–2008.* New York: Oxford University Press. Also http://hdr.undp.org/en/reports/

global/hdr2007–2008/. (Additional reports can be accessed using this link and inserting the year you wish to access.)

VeneKlasen, Lisa, and Valerie Miller. 2002. *A New Weave of Power, People, and Politics: The Action Guide for Advocacy and Citizen Participation.* Oklahoma City: World Neighbors.